—— *A Culinary History of* ——

MONTGOMERY
COUNTY
MARYLAND

A Culinary History of

MONTGOMERY COUNTY
MARYLAND

CLAUDIA KOUSOULAS AND ELLEN LETOURNEAU

AMERICAN PALATE

Published by American Palate
A Division of The History Press
Charleston, SC
www.historypress.com

Copyright © 2022 by Claudia Kousoulas and Ellen Letourneau
All rights reserved

First published 2022

Manufactured in the United States

ISBN 9781467148658

Library of Congress Control Number: 2022930164

Notice: The information in this book is true and complete to the best of our knowledge. It is offered without guarantee on the part of the authors or The History Press. The authors and The History Press disclaim all liability in connection with the use of this book.

CONTENTS

CONTENTS

ACKNOWLEDGEMENTS

*W*e are very fortunate that Montgomery County has many residents who are passionate about the county's history, development, lands and future, and we are grateful that they shared their work and knowledge with us.

Greg Brown, Maryland Historical Trust
Jim and Tina Brown
Patrick Butler, M-NCPPC
Julie Clendenin, Calleva
Anthony Cohen, Button Farm
Matthew Cohen, Matt's Habitats
Kevin Davey, M-NCPPC
Katie Dishman, Marriott International
Garner W. Duvall, Mooseum
Jeanne Gartner
Barbara Grunbaum
Sarah Hedlund, Montgomery History
Shelley Heron, Mooseum
Derek Jackson, Sandy Spring Museum Archives
Suzanne Johnson, Sugarland Ethnohistory Project
Christopher Knowles
George Kousoulas
Catie Leonard

ACKNOWLEDGEMENTS

George McDaniel
Barbara McGraw, Mooseum
Jessica McVary, M-NCPPC
Cassandra Michaud, Montgomery County Parks Archaeology
Michelle Nelson, M-NCPPC—Montgomery Parks
Kara Piccirilli, Charles Koiner Conservancy
Enoch Pratt Library/Digital Maryland
Christine Rai, Frederick Community College
Richard Rowe
Patricia Samford, Maryland Archaeological Conservation Lab, Jefferson Patterson Park and Museum
Hannah Sholder, Charles Koiner Conservancy
John B. Stock, Stock Nursery
Tara Tetrault, Montgomery College
Piera Weiss
Sandi Williams, Sandy Spring Slave Museum & African Art Gallery Inc.
Christine Hill Wilson, Women's Board Medstar Montgomery Medical Center, Olney, MD

INTRODUCTION

At the table, different members of the family meet, and where affection and kindness, those aids to true politeness, preside, it is truly a delightful treat to be the guest of such a family.
—*Elizabeth Ellicott Lea,* Domestic Cookery

Montgomery County stands between—between the Tidewater and the Piedmont, between north and south, between the urbanity of the national capital and the rural preserved lands of its Agricultural Reserve, between the Maryland ways of Baltimore and the Tidewater and the international ways of Washington. It stands between urban and rural in its own decision to create an Agricultural Reserve. Together, these form the county's unique character, some of which is reflected at the table.

Food and foodways—how we produce, prepare and share food—reflect culture at nearly every level: social life, technology, economy, environment and more. Food can also be used to tell the stories of history that we see cycle through generations—in the attention to transportation infrastructure, the parceling out of land and thus opportunity, the care given to soils, the urge to adopt technology, the requirement for power and energy sources and people building communities and recording their histories.

The earliest records of county history describe the land as a fundamental value, addressing its character, quality, location and suitable uses. We see that same interest in current farmers' attention to soil quality, recognizing

Rocklands Farm Winery. *Courtesy George Kousoulas.*

that fertile soil is the source of their produce, as well as community decisions about development.

We also see an attention to local markets. Early farmers grew for export, and when the market for tobacco crashed, they were left with depleted soils. Over time, Montgomery produce has shifted from grain to beef to dairy and is now a mix of commodity crops, table crops and value-added farm products. And just as early residents were drawn to sightseeing at the Potomac's falls and lunch under the trees at country inns, today's residents still enjoy the county's national and state parks as well as its wineries, breweries and u-pick farms.

Technology has always played a role in Montgomery's foodways. The Sandy Spring farm community was instrumental in developing farming techniques in soil restoration, livestock breeding and plant varieties, as well as equipment like an early refrigerator and more efficient plows. Even an eggbeater influenced the county's development.

Montgomery County has always been a diverse place, and although that diversity has shifted over time, it includes stories of the first Columbian encounters, the exploitation of enslaved labor and the labor of indentured servants. Early settlers brought German, English, southern and native influences to the table. In more recent times, Montgomery has taken on

Rocklands Farm Winery. *Courtesy George Kousoulas.*

One Acre Farm. *Courtesy George Kousoulas.*

In *The History of Montgomery County, Maryland from Its Earliest Settlement, 1650 to 1879*, T.H.S. Boyd presented the county in the way that beach town chamber of commerce maps highlight fudge shops and tour bus depots—a partial picture but a vivid one. He describes in detail what would otherwise be lost—the types of peaches grown and when they fruit, carriages lined up outside grocery establishments and the confectionery shop's marble slabs where the molasses is spread to cool—always emphasizing the excellence of the product, the geniality of citizens and the undeniably bright future of the community.

He declares that "the mantel of sire fell on worthy shoulders" and describes heroic businessmen, tireless land clearers, the expense and handsomeness of the buildings, the progress of development and the ability to expand and compete. There are stories of businessmen who start with five dollars and, thanks to ambition, prudence and determination, take hold of the American opportunity.

We think differently now, measuring success by a more careful husbanding of resources, a more cautious use of precious land and a more knowing view of who is able to achieve, but we can take pride in what stewardship has created.

Washington, D.C.'s international character with immigrant communities and their cultures, including food.

And through time, we can trace the symbiotic economy created by land use, transportation, industry and markets—from farmland to suburbanization, from canal to highways, from mills to microchips and from wagonloads to truckloads.

Food can tell all these stories.

AMONG THE MOST SIGNIFICANT decisions in shaping Montgomery County's development and its foodways was the creation of an Agricultural Reserve in 1980. In the national capital region, land is always at a premium, yet Montgomery County chose to set aside one-third of its land, ninety-three thousand acres, for agricultural uses.

In the Reserve, you can head to one of the farms for apples and pumpkins in the fall and keep an eye on the calendar for summer corn and strawberries.

Linden Farm. *Courtesy George Kousoulas.*

You can hike along the C&O Canal and marvel at the rock formations along the Potomac River or bike along rising and falling rustic roads. These pastoral and natural scenes are the results of hours of planning, research and analysis, repeated and sometimes contentious public meetings and tough political decisions.

Farm visits and canal hikes only scratch the surface of what the Reserve offers. The intention and actions taken to preserve farming also preserved historic sites, a diverse economy and the natural environment, including the water supply for the 4 million people who live in the capital region. The Reserve offers education, recreation, beauty and inspiration.

While this book tells stories of local, historical foodways that range from canalboats and riverfront hotels, from kitchens of the owned and the owners and of farm women who cooked their convictions and took their biscuits to the bank, the book's underlying message is that there is no local food—the summer strawberries and crisp apples—without local land. The decision to preserve farming in Montgomery County was made decades ago, but it is one that we all must protect by advocating for farmland with decision-makers, by understanding the challenges to local farming and even by taking a hike or picking an apple.

MONTGOMERY COUNTY TIMELINE

1608   Captain John Smith encounters native Piscataways.

1609   Henry Spelman begins trading with Native Americans.

1625   Henry Fleet navigates the Potomac and is taken captive.

1634   Maryland is established at St. Mary's City.

1700s   Montgomery County land grants are mapped, and Native Americans are pushed off their lands.

1715   Scottish refugees arrive in Montgomery County, "despairing of the fortunes of the House of Stuart."

1748   The area that is now Montgomery County is carved out from Prince George's County as part of Frederick County.

1751   Georgetown land is purchased to establish a port community.

1765   The British Parliament passes the Stamp Act to levy taxes and exert its power over American colonies.

1774   A meeting at the Hungerford Tavern in Rockville resolves to support Boston amid the British blockade of its port.

Staub's Lunch offered "Home Made Cakes & Pies." The original business was owned by Charlie Staub's parents after they sold cars and began selling sandwiches from a window. After his parents left the business, Charlie and his wife opened the small restaurant for breakfast and lunch where he used a flat grill to make hamburgers. He would go to Selby's market daily to get fresh ground beef and used an old ice cream scoop to measure out the burger patties. They were known for their burgers, and when the business was sold in 1980, the new owners offered a Charley Burger in his honor. *Courtesy Montgomery History.*

1776   Montgomery County is established, named for Revolutionary War hero Richard Montgomery.

1782   The county's population is 10,011 White and 4,407 Black.

1784   The Potomac Company is established to build a canal to create a river trade route.

1786   The boundary is established between Prince George's and Montgomery Counties.

1787   Georgetown is incorporated as a city.

1790   The federal government establishes a permanent capital.

1791   Georgetown is ceded by Maryland to become part of the national capital.

1798   Montgomery County is divided into election districts.

1799   The first record of a farmer's club in Sandy Spring.

1801   Rockville is established with a courthouse.

1807   The Board of Agriculture is established.

1808   The town of Brookeville is laid out.

1811   A Maryland General Assembly act prescribes a penalty for "erecting booths or selling liquor within two miles of any Methodist camp or quarterly meeting."

1817   An act is passed to prevent geese and swine from going at large in or within a quarter mile of Rockville.

1823   The federal government funds a survey of a proposed canal route.

Edgar Dove grew up in the kinship community of Scotland and worked at the Bethesda A&P. In an oral history, he recalled, "There used to be a place, a restaurant there, it was called Agnew's, and we used to go there a lot. When we went to Agnew's, we had to go around the parking lot of the restaurant and go around in the back door. We'd go in sometime and get a six-pack of beer, go there sometime and buy us a hamburger or a ham sandwich or something like that. You couldn't go in the front door." *Courtesy Montgomery History.*

1828   The C&O Canal and B&O Railroad both break ground on July 4.

Construction of Great Falls Tavern begins, and it is designated as Lockhouse 12.

1830   The county's population is 19,816.

Great Falls Tavern is enlarged at the cost of $200 to add a kitchen.

Canal construction reaches Cabin John; Lockhouse 8 is built.

1831   The C&O Canal reaches from Georgetown to Seneca.

1833   George Chichester is authorized to operate a ferry from his lands in Virginia across the Potomac River.

An act is passed to restrain the sale of "ardent spirits" in Brookeville.

The C&O Canal reaches from Seneca to Harper's Ferry, West Virginia.

1839   The C&O Canal reaches from Harpers Ferry, West Virginia, to Hancock, Maryland.

1840   The county's population drops to 15,456 as many leave behind spent farms.

1845   Elizabeth Ellicott Lea's *Domestic Cookery, Useful Receipts, and Hints to Young Housekeepers* is published.

1846   The Montgomery County Agricultural Society is established to run the Rockville Agricultural Fair.

1848   Great Falls Tavern, also known as Crommelin House, is prohibited from selling intoxicating liquor.

1849   Great Falls Tavern is no longer rented as a commercial use but is instead used as a lockhouse.

Josiah Henson publishes his autobiography to earn money to purchase his brother's freedom.

1850   The C&O Canal reaches from Hancock to Cumberland, Maryland, and in October opens for its entire length.

There are 1,051 farms operating in the county.

1851   The Great Falls Tavern's ballroom is used as a grocery store.

Harriet Beecher Stowe's *Uncle Tom's Cabin* is published as a serial.

1857   Construction of Union Arch Bridge aqueduct begins.

1858   Great Falls Tavern is reestablished as a hotel or ordinary "for the accommodation of visitors."

1861   The Civil War begins, and martial law is declared in Montgomery County.

1862   Enslaved people are emancipated in Washington, D.C.

1863   Enslaved people are emancipated in seceded states, but not in Maryland, which never seceded.

1864   Enslaved people are emancipated in Maryland.

1865   The Emancipation Proclamation is issued, and the Civil War ends.

1870   Rosa and Joseph Bobinger construct the Cabin John Bridge Hotel.

1871   Congress repeals Georgetown's charter as an independent municipality.

1873   The Olney Grange is established.

The B&O Railroad opens the Metropolitan Branch from Washington, D.C., to Frederick, Maryland.

1874   The Agricultural Society is incorporated.

1878   Gaithersburg is incorporated.

1888   The Rock Creek Railway Company is incorporated by Francis Newlands, opening Chevy Chase to suburban development.

1891   The historic Rockville Courthouse is built.

1890   The Chevy Chase Land Company buys land to develop a suburban community.

1892   The trolley from Connecticut Avenue and 18th Street, NW, opens to Chevy Chase Lake.

1897   The *Up-to-Date Cookbook* is published.

Food is often an entry into American business for immigrant groups. The District Grocery Store on the 7400 block of Wisconsin Avenue in Bethesda was one of the individually owned and operated stores that bought and advertised collectively. The cooperative began in 1921, and most of the one-room stores were run by Jewish families looking for a business foothold. The cooperative offered home delivery but also self-service, as later supermarkets would. *Courtesy M-NCPPC.*

1909   The Negro Agricultural Fair is held in Sandy Spring.

1910   Since 1890, Bethesda has tripled and Wheaton doubled their respective populations.

1912   Land is purchased to build the Cabin John Park subdivision.

1917   The United States enters World War I.

1924   A massive March flood ends hauling on the C&O Canal.

1927   J. Willard Marriott opens his first Hot Shoppes restaurant in Washington, D.C.

1931   Cabin John Bridge Hotel burns down.

1935   There are 1,900 farms in the county.

1937   First Montgomery County Hot Shoppes opens in Chevy Chase.

1938   The C&O Canal is acquired by Department of the Interior.

1939   Of the county's 319,160 acres, 69.2 percent are in farms.

The C&O Canal is designated as a public park.

1940   The county's population is 83,912, with an assessable tax base of $147 million.

1941   The United States enters World War II.

1948   A new charter establishes a county manager and home rule (after repeated efforts starting in 1936).

1949   67.4 percent of county land is in farms.

The Montgomery County Agricultural Center Inc. is established in Gaithersburg to operate the fairgrounds.

1950   Georgetown is designated as a historic district.

The county's population is 164,401 (nearly doubled in ten years), with an assessable tax base of $483 million.

There are 1,555 farms operating in the county.

1951   Great Falls Tavern opens as a museum.

1954   The C&O Canal is proposed as the site of an extension of the George Washington Memorial Parkway.

Justice William O. Douglas hikes the canal to bring public attention to its natural beauty.

The A&P national grocery chain grew by selling no-frills groceries and eventually added produce and meat. The company set up self-service stores, manufactured its own products and accommodated shoppers who were driving cars. The chain began to decline in the 1950s, as its modern ideas of distribution and service were adopted and expanded by even larger retailers offering more variety. *Courtesy M-NCPPC.*

1955   Marriott opens its headquarters building at 5161 River Road in Bethesda.

1960   The county's population is 213,721 (a 30 percent increase in ten years), with an assessable tax base of $1 billion.

There are nine hundred farms operating in the county.

1961   County schools are integrated ("Negro schools" began closing in 1955).

1963   *Maryland's Way* cookbook is published.

1971   The C&O Canal is declared a national historic park.

1979   New Marriott headquarters opens off of Fernwood Road, in an office campus that was a former dairy farm.

1980   The county adopts the Agricultural and Open Space Master Plan, establishing a ninety-three-thousand-acre Agricultural Reserve.

1995   The Bethesda Hot Shoppes closes.

MONTGOMERY COUNTY POPULATION

1790	18,003
1800	15,058
1810	17,980
1820	16,400
1830	19,816
1840	15,456
1850	15,860
1860	18,322
1870	20,563
1880	24,759
1890	27,185
1900	30,451
1910	32,089

1920	34,921
1930	49,206 (40 percent increase)
1940	83,912 (70 percent increase)
1950	164,401 (95 percent increase)
1960	340,928 (107 percent increase)
1970	522,809
1980	579,953
1990	757,027
2000	873,341
2010	971,777
2020	1,050,688 (estimate)

Chapter 1

ESTABLISHING THE AGRICULTURAL RESERVE

*W*e often drive by open land and think it's empty, undeveloped, vacant. But hovering unseen over that land is a web of public and private decisions that shapes the health of the soil, what can be extracted from the property, what can be built on it and, because of those things, its monetary value. These decisions about land use, planning and infrastructure are designed to build communities and protect public health, safety and welfare, but they often have spin-off effects. In the case of Montgomery County's Agricultural Reserve, those effects are local food, local economy and local history.

Setting aside one-third of the county for agriculture and open space was a bold act of stewardship undertaken through a rigorous public process of research, planning and community participation. The Reserve's ninety-three thousand acres, in the rapidly developing national capital area, could have easily been lost to suburban development. Instead, this land has preserved air and water quality, the natural environment, jobs, local food and history.

In his 1879 history, T.H.S. Boyd recorded the nations of indigenous peoples at the time of first settlement in 1635—"Yoacomicos, Anacostians, Piscataways, Senecas and Patuxents" who would give their names to regions and communities that were later taken over by European settlers.

Both the native populations and the settlers were drawn to the Potomac, which has been variously translated from the Algonkian language as "where something is brought," "something brought" and "trading place." The river was a source of water, a good hunting ground and a means of transportation—resources necessary to any successful community. The river remains a defining feature in the Washington region.

The initial land grants would be divided to create a farm economy focused not on towns but on adjacent estates that would eventually be further divided into smaller farms and into housing lots as the region developed.

In 1776, with a growing population, Montgomery County was carved out of Frederick County and, in patriotic fervor, named for Richard Montgomery, a fallen general of the Revolutionary War battles at Quebec and Montreal. As the site of the national capital, development would continue in the region, but Montgomery remained a farm economy through the Civil War.

The county's landscape, population and economy began to change most noticeably at the turn of the nineteenth century. In 1873, the Metropolitan Branch railway from the District to Frederick would connect farms along its route to markets. In 1888, the Rock Creek Railway was incorporated from the District to Chevy Chase Lake and, in its wake, turned farms into suburban communities. Georgetown was incorporated as a city at the end of the 1780s, but in 1791, it lost its charter and title and was absorbed into the city of Washington. In the 1920s, a massive flood would end the commercial operations of the C&O Canal. The systems and infrastructure of Montgomery's farm communities and economy were changing as the region changed.

Although much of Montgomery County was agricultural, even into the early twentieth century, postwar development was further changing the county's character, its economy and the value of its land. Two national security decisions drove suburban development by relocating jobs and the means to reach them. The Eisenhower National System of Interstate and Defense Highways was authorized by the 1956 Federal Highway Act. Although earlier federal road building efforts had started to build a network, a national system was championed by Eisenhower, who as a young officer had crossed the country in the 1919 Motor Transport Corps and, later, as commander of Allied forces in Europe, was influenced by Germany's autobahn system. The committee he appointed in the 1950s noted that a highway system public works project was necessary for defense and the economy.

In Montgomery County, I-270, from the District north to Frederick, and the Beltway, the I-95 route around the city, would draw development into the county's northern reaches, making some land more valuable for development than for farming.

The second decision was decentralizing federal government agencies. From its initial days, the federal government operated in a somewhat decentralized way—the executive and legislative at opposite ends of Pennsylvania Avenue is a physical expression of the separation of powers. During and after World War II, the federal government's operations expanded, and a new law expanded the notion of the "District" in Article 1 of the Constitution to extend beyond the originally ceded ten square miles, that in fact, the Washington metropolitan region—its surrounding counties in Maryland and Virginia—were a contemporary version of the "capital of ten miles square." There were economic arguments, national security arguments and practical arguments for more space.

In Montgomery County, the population increased tenfold between 1920 and 1960, when development pressure really reached into the up-county. Federal government expansions and transportation infrastructure changed the way land was used and valued. In 1955, the Atomic Energy Commission came to the county, and in 1960, planning for the regional Metrorail system began. In 1961, the National Institute of Standards and Technology moved to Gaithersburg and would be easily reachable via the Beltway, which opened in 1964. By 1978, Montgomery County would have its first Metrorail station.

Writing in 1961's *In Old Homes and History of Montgomery County, Maryland*, Roger Brooke Farquhar noted, "Suburbanization of the county with the rapid expansion of the Nation's Capital is continuing apace. Where stately fields of wheat once stood there are now trim new homes by the thousands and farmlands are constantly being erased as the perimeter of the suburbs is extended."

In 1969, Martha Sprigg Poole, editor of the *Montgomery County Story*, recalled summer visits to her grandparents' county farm, where she "learned what the job of farming was like." Poole captured her memories as the landscape and economy she described was disappearing. She was concerned that growing up in the suburbs, "[y]oung people today have almost no opportunity to visit a working farm in Montgomery County. The City has expanded so that Housing Developments, Shopping Malls, High-rise Apartments, huge Government Installations and other office buildings now occupy almost all the land that 50 years ago was used for farming."

Law Watkins and his neighbors could also see that the coming change would bring the end of farming in the county. His family had farmed in the county for generations, and he recalled that his mother had a particularly good eye for land—"A remarkable sense." His family bought the farm to raise cattle but switched to organic wheat and had a few years of "agricultural peace." In 1969, things started to change; there was more traffic and development. Knowing that "farming is fragile," Watkins put his land into an easement that would limit it to agricultural uses and convinced some of his abutting neighbors to do the same.

The easements limited the use of the land to agriculture. Without development potential, the land would generate a lower sales price and thus warrant a lower tax bill. Lower taxes and limited uses kept land in active farming and made it easier to pass down as a working farm. It was an active stewardship intended to support "real farming, real care of the land, and a real economy." In combination with the Rustic Roads program, started by noted planner and historian Frederick Gutheim, the initial 1,600-acre block of land was an important early move toward stewardship of farmland in the county.

In its 1964 General Plan, the county established a development pattern that recognized the varied character of land and the resources—roads and public sewer and water—that served it. The "Wedges and Corridors" plan sought to create a defined landscape in which development and public investment could be directed and managed under a larger vision. In his book *Suburb*, Royce Hanson, who was planning board chairman at the time, wrote that the wedges and corridors were "more aspiration than policy," noting that the pattern "was complicated by reality."

Part of that reality was a 1970s sewer moratorium, which limited new building connections to existing water and sewer service. But demand was strong and pushed development to large lot sites that could be served by well and septic systems. As part of the change observed by Law Watkins, development was starting to nibble at the edges of agricultural land, "fragmenting the rural landscape," wrote Hanson.

Pressure to lift the building moratorium also increased, and a proposal for a new wastewater treatment plant was proposed by WSSC (the regional water and sewer authority), endorsed by the county executive and supported by the development community. As Hanson noted, it would have opened the western wedge to development, and so the County Planning Department quickly drafted a rural zone with a five-acre minimum lot size.

As a basis for the rezoning, planners compiled, analyzed and mapped zoning, land use, tax records, property ownership, municipal jurisdictions, soils and other information to identify properties that should be rezoned into the proposed rural zone.

Mapping also identified areas without sewer service and areas where little development had occurred—an area of 163,000 acres, about half the county. Also mapped were soils, working farms and land assessed as farms, existing and planned parkland, floodplains, lands along the Potomac

River and C&O Canal, reservoirs and conservation areas surrounding Sugarloaf Mountain.

The maps revealed about 110,000 acres, with most of the county's farmland that arced along the northern portion of the county from the Potomac River to the Patuxent River. The area included towns and villages that were centers for the rural community—Poolesville, Laytonsville, Barnesville, Damascus, Boyds, Dickerson, Woodfield, Unity and Sunshine. The Rural Zone and eventually the Agricultural Reserve would end up covering more than one-third of the county.

Land takes its value from what it can be used for. A property may have value as a mining site or provide access to water. It might be located in a busy downtown or may have fertile soil. Perhaps it spans a road or railroad line that provides access but also can be decked over and built on. These are land-use rights, often referred to as a "bundle of sticks"—remove any one of those sticks and the others remain. But those rights are mediated by decisions made for the public health, safety and welfare—mining your property may cause subsidence on your neighbor's. Zoning is a tool of mediation, ensuring public health, safety and welfare, as well as determining a land-use pattern that can ensure public investment is in the public interest. It directs development and, by doing so, makes some land more valuable than others.

The proposed Rural Zone for the northern third of Montgomery County was a downzoning. Before the rezoning, a farmer could build five houses on twenty-five acres. Afterward, he could build just one house on those twenty-five acres. He had lost the value of four house lots, which, in a growing metropolitan region, could be significant.

This rezoning—a technical planning solution based on research and mapping—wasn't sufficient by itself. It had to run the gamut of political decision-making, which in Montgomery County is an intense process requiring meetings and public hearings. Property owners and abutters had to be notified by mail, and ads were run in local newspapers. Hanson recalled that civic and business organizations were included, and meetings were held, sometimes at kitchen tables, with community and neighborhood groups.

Planners and politicians heard significant pushback from those who thought the county was taking their equity, overstepping its bounds and acting to harm. In response, planners argued that the real value came not from the number of houses allowed by zoning but from the number of houses that could be supported by a well and septic system—a number that was about one house per five acres, what the Rural Zone proposed—"the reality of what the land could support without sewer service."

Many remained unconvinced that farming had value and viewed the Rural Zone as merely a "holding zone" until inevitable development became worthwhile. Farming in Montgomery County seemed antiquated and not part of a future economy. Beyond zoning, there needed to be a plan, based on a larger concept of land use, that would preserve agriculture. The plan needed to determine which land was worth saving, a pattern that would create a critical mass of agricultural land, and a way to capture some of the land value lost in the rezoning.

The 1980 Agriculture and Open Space Plan solved those problems and developed a guiding concept: the Agricultural Reserve. Hanson noted that the Reserve was named to convey the message that this was a place for active farming, and beyond zoning, to "create an image of uniqueness justifying continuing stewardship." The goal was to preserve not just open space, but the farming that gives the land an economic anchor.

Land also takes value from access, and the 1980 plan addressed transportation issues that would have drastically changed the Reserve's character and function. Life and property in Washington (and, in some matters, by the rest of the country) is defined as inside the Beltway and outside the Beltway. In Montgomery County, inside the Beltway are dense urban and suburban communities; outside are the county's more rural areas. A proposed Outer Beltway, a highway continuation of I-95, intended to connect via a new bridge over the Potomac to Virginia's Loudoun County and Dulles Airport, was drawn as a line on a planning map—indicating an intention that hadn't yet been pursued with engineering or funding.

Where a highway goes, development follows, so the line had to be erased. As Hanson wrote, it had been approved in segments and would be removed the same way. A decline in gas tax revenue prompted Maryland to remove it from the state highway program, and in 1980, a local plan for the Potomac community, along the river, removed the western segment. The eastern segment would be built to connect Routes I-95 and 1 and to Baltimore-Washington Thurgood Marshall Airport.

The research for the Rural Zone had determined that the northern third of the county was agriculturally feasible and would create a critical mass of land for a farm economy, although there were, and sometimes and still are, conflicts between farmers and their slow tractors and sometimes smelly or noisy operations and those who enjoy the Reserve for its view.

A key tool in recouping lost land values for rezoned farmland was Transferable Development Rights (TDRs), which treats property rights as a bundle of sticks, removing one of the sticks—the right to develop—and

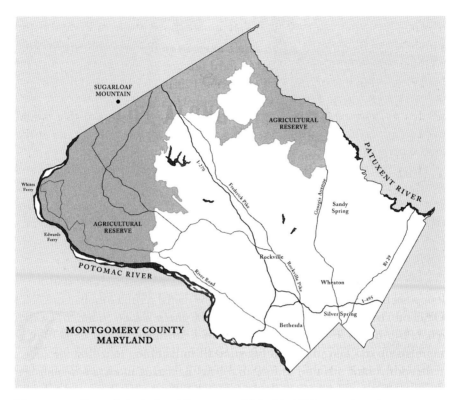

Montgomery County's Agricultural Reserve, established in 1980, comprises ninety-three thousand acres of parks, trails and historic sites, as well as a variety of agricultural businesses including farm stands, orchards, u-pick farms, table crops and commodity crops, vineyards and breweries. *Courtesy George Kousoulas.*

allowing the sale of that right, transferred to another property. It was an idea borrowed from the preservation of Grand Central Station. The station was kept in place, while its "air rights," the right to develop in the space above the station, were sold and transferred to other properties.

In Montgomery County, TDRs from farmland could be sold to developers in Silver Spring or Bethesda, where the county had invested public money in roads, schools, parks, transit and other public facilities that could support increased development. Bethesda and Silver Spring were transformed into active, varied suburban downtowns, and farmland remained farmable.

It was a tool that made farming possible. Butler's, a successful u-pick operation, was looking to expand but couldn't afford the land adjacent to its Davis Mill Road farm, which was priced to redevelop. It was looking at land in Pennsylvania, until the Rural Zone made abutting land affordable. Wade Butler recalled that their neighbor wasn't happy about the rezoning, which

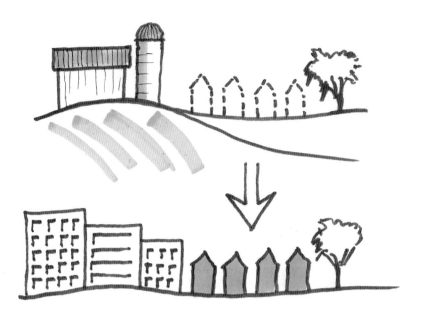

Transferable Development Rights, or TDRs, are a zoning tool used to direct development across a region. Sending areas are the source of development rights that can be used in receiving areas, which have the infrastructure needed to support buildings, people and activity. *Courtesy George Kousoulas.*

reduced his value, but they eventually developed a relationship and he even helped them with business advice.

TDRs were a market-based solution that captured cash value for the farmer and development value for a developer. Hanson noted that their success in Montgomery County came from being based in a master plan with a strong concept, zoning designed to support the program with a balance of sending and receiving areas that created a strong market for sale and purchase, and that their operation was simple—minimal cost and paperwork. It was an early use of TDRs and one of the largest that has been a model for both case studies and other communities.

The Reserve also takes its strength from the fact that it is not primarily public land. As such, its continuation requires that policy, politics and private decisions pull together. It is the hard work of stewardship. Advocacy groups like the Montgomery Countryside Alliance, Equestrian Partners in Conservation, Sugarloaf Conservancy, the Sugarloaf Citizens Association and Montgomery Agricultural Producers each come to the Reserve with their own perspective, seeking literal and figurative common ground.

Like many large efforts, the Reserve has required refinements and adjustments over time. As Hanson noted in a talk for the organization Montgomery History, the 1980 plan limited development by not allowing alternative sewage technologies, but once sand mounds were declared standard, they prompted new development. The Building Lot Termination easement program was established in 2008 to combat land fragmentation through development. As with TDRs, land value is captured by reselling the easement's value for development elsewhere in the county.

The Reserve's large properties were attractive to private institutional facilities looking to build campus-like developments, but they didn't support agriculture and generated large amounts of traffic. This was addressed when the County Planning Board limited such facilities to five thousand gallons/day of sewer used and no public water. Likewise, they were not allowed on TDR easement land.

We often think it inevitable that cities will overtake the countryside, viewing it as a mark of progress and opportunity or, as land-use attorneys say, the land's "highest and best use." But in fact, the city and countryside are interdependent. As historian Lewis Mumford wrote in the 1930s, "Every phase of life in the countryside contributes to the existence of cities."

Today, the Agricultural Reserve supports the Washington metropolitan region with many of the things we value. It is the source of the region's backup drinking water supply—an insurance policy of clean water for more than 4 million residents. It is a place for recreation and respite. Weekend walkers can enjoy the combination of man-made and natural environment that makes the C&O Canal a unique national park. Flocks of cyclists, heads down and legs churning, sweep along the Reserve's historic rustic roads. At farms, gardens and in the natural landscape, people can step out of the everyday to find peace and beauty.

At particular times of the year, horseback riders will gather for an annual hunt and summer campers marshal their gear for canoe trips and campfires. Families drive out for pumpkins, Christmas trees, sour cherries and strawberries, creating annual traditions.

Local jobs shift with the seasons. CSA and farm stand farmers take tentative steps with their customers in the spring with the first greens and berries, anticipating the summer and fall bounty. Wineries and breweries welcome visitors for local produce suppers or simply for a glass of wine and a view. Artisans and artisanal products like honey and lavender bloom in their season.

School trips, farm tours and history weekends are a chance to learn about green building or organic farming, to experience lessons in a one-room schoolhouse, to trace the path of the Underground Railroad through the county or mark the single day when the town of Brookeville served as the nation's capital.

The Reserve is an environment of diversity—a canvas that is unique land in the region. Summer jobs serving customers or setting strawberry plants can lead to careers. The economy it creates offers jobs. Not everyone wants to sit in front of a screen, and work in the Reserve ranges from hospitality to the varied skills required to be a successful farmer. On any given day, a farmer may be required to be a mechanic, veterinarian, botanist, banker, climatologist, entomologist and more.

There is also a diversity of people who farm and the ways they farm, from individual farmers on small "land-link" plots to large farms handed down through families. They grow commodity crops that are shipped out of the county for processing, they grow table crops of seasonal food and they create unique value-added products. This local market basket is priced at a premium, but it's worth the drive and extra cost because it preserves land and jobs. The produce is also shared with neighbors in need through programs like the Manna Food Center, which partners with markets and farmers. These diverse landholders, interests and groups come together, with different points of view, but are involved in creating their community.

Over time, the people who come to Montgomery County have diversified. Native peoples had a wide-ranging diet from foraging, hunting, fishing and agriculture. Early English, Scotch-Irish and German settlers adapted their traditions—pies, wheat breads and fruit butters—to local produce like corn and apples. In the late nineteenth and early twentieth centuries, the county offered recreation that included food—either from hotel French-inspired menus or inns offering southern-style hospitality. Today, Montgomery residents bring international traditions from Asia, India and South America to local tables.

Farming has also shifted over time. Original settlers relied on Indians to supply them with corn that would help them survive. Early farms ranged from diversified farmsteads that produced a mix of crops for sale and home use to cash crop tobacco plantations. As the market changed, so did farm production, from wheat and cattle to dairy. Today, farms grow grapes at wineries, table crops for CSAs and commodity crops for market.

The connection between food and history is tied to the way we think about food now: local and seasonal. It's an attitude that describes a luxury but was once a matter of survival. As culinary historian Michael Twitty noted, food production moved through phases with the year. In the spring,

Sugarloaf Mountain marks Montgomery County's border with Frederick County. It was noted by early settlers, was a Civil War lookout point and today is still a place surrounded by the farm fields of the Agricultural Reserve. *Courtesy Montgomery History.*

it was time to plant cool weather crops, net spawning fish and collect wild greens. Summer offered catfish and perch, a wheat harvest, sweet corn and other garden vegetables and fruit. Fall was the time to store this harvest for a winter of banked crops and preserved produce.

Today, the Reserve offers a connection to that seasonality. Families make trips to pick apples or berries, spring is marked with Bunnyland at Butler's Orchard and the annual Thanksgiving hunt provides a picture of history. But the Reserve has the potential to provide even more local and seasonal food. As Royce Hanson, a former planning board chairman who can certainly be called the father of the Reserve, pointed out, policies to support food farming to meet local demand is the kind of active farming envisioned when the Reserve was established—a beautiful place and a productive place.

Chapter 2

TWO VIEWS OF LAND

*L*ands along the Potomac River were the site of numerous native settlements—agricultural communities connected by trails that would eventually become the county's oldest thoroughfares, whose people fished in streams that would become mill sites, hunting and farming on lands that would be divided into land grants and later into suburban subdivisions.

The Conoy Federation numbered at least six tribal groups—including Pamunkies, Piscataways, Anacostans, Nanticokes and Powhatans—and while they relied on the area's natural bounty for survival, their attitude toward the land was one of balance, not extraction. They viewed land as the source of culture and identity, a connection that went beyond ownership, into stewardship. It is a relationship that some might dismiss as romantic, perhaps because the connection can't be easily valued in the marketplace.

The Potomac was a gathering and trading place, and archaeological excavations have found various sites of established settlements. Four archaeological sites have been excavated and recorded. The Hughes, Winslow, Shepard and Selden Island sites are among the sites of the county's first residents. The sites are mostly Late Woodland (circa AD 1300) villages, and while they have at times been looted and destroyed by the C&O Canal construction, the findings reveal day-to-day and season-to-season life. Along with burial sites, evidence of structures and hearth and pit sites, the middens reveal clay ceramic sherds, tempered with granite and quartz, some with flat bottoms and others with conical bottoms, as well as occasionally decorated with incised markings. Food remains include corncobs and kernels, hickory nuts, beans, wild fruits, fungi and animal bone.

But the people moved through the land with the season, having "no permanent residence within county borders," according to T.H.S. Boyd. They lived in seasonally occupied camps, near a bountiful resource, water areas for game, fish runs and foraging grounds. Henry Fleet, an early European navigator of the Potomac River, in 1625 described the country as abounding in game, such as deer, buffalos, bears and turkeys, while the river abounded in all kinds of fish—"the Indians commonly catching thirty sturgeon in one night."

The native groups shifted their settlements and community patterns to follow winter and summer hunting and fishing grounds, and pre-contact, the land offered an array of foods, including game, fish, mollusks, shellfish, nuts, seeds and wild grains. Deer furnished meat as well as hides for clothing and bone for tools. Other small mammals were also likely part of the diet. While vegetable remains decompose, pit remains have revealed corn, squash and hickory nuts as food staples. Persimmons and pawpaw grew and still grow in the area's forests.

In *Eating in America*, Waverly Root begins by pointing out that we often view Native American cooking as a survivalist effort, a poor collection of acorns and insects—"the white man has always liked to believe that the Indian dwelt in a state of perpetual misery until Europeans arrived to improve his condition." He speculates that at the time of contact, indigenous people were eating better than the average European, with a wider variety and more equitable distribution of food, cooked "with considerable finesse" and served following codes of politeness and equity.

On that table were potatoes, onions, sunflower, wild leeks and garlic, a variety of root and tubers, hickory nuts, beechnuts, hazelnuts, chestnuts, black walnuts and butternuts. Acorns were processed into flour and oil. Root went on to describe bay plants, berries, greens, fruits, beans and cereals that were made into dishes to accompany the game.

A variety of foraged plants was also used medicinally, and T.H.S. Boyd recorded "rattlesnake root, the skins of rattlesnakes dried and pulverized, thorny ash, toothache tree, tulip tree, dogwood, wild laurel, sassafras, elder, poison ash, wintergreen, liverwort, Virginia poke, jalap, sarsaparilla, Scobians or devil's bit, blood wort, cuckoopint, and others."

While some native foods were found across regions, foodways were based in local environments that naturally created regional variety; as Root wrote,

BLACK WALNUTS are native to eastern North America and can be found throughout Montgomery County, in forests and along roadsides. Unlike commercially sold, thin-shelled English walnuts, black walnuts are small, encased by a green husk and a hard black shell. Remnants of the hard shells are often found in Native American archaeological sites and can be used as a dye. In *Domestic Cookery*, Elizabeth Ellicott Lea includes recipes for blue, red, yellow and green dyes using natural ingredients. "To Dye Brown," she prescribes "young walnuts with the leaves and bark" layered with wool, weighted and left to soak for a week. The result is "a pretty brown that will not fade." The husks fall in August and must be spread to dry before they can be removed. The hard inner shell has to be cracked with a rock or hammer and the nut picked out from a chambered inner space. After that work, the nut has a distinct flavor, slightly fruity, described by some as sweet and strong.

there is "as much difference between an Algonquin and a Hopi as between a Swede and an Italian."

Along with foraging and hunting, Root pointed out that Native Americans also grew a wider variety of plants than the settling Europeans had done and used farming methods adapted to the environment. In the Southwest, bat guano was used as fertilizer, while fish was used in the Northeast. Native farmers developed irrigation techniques and adapted wild plants for cultivation. In fact, early European corn crops failed when the seeds were planted by scattering, rather than by the Indian method of fertilized hills. Corn and beans were grown together because beans fix nitrogen in their roots (they also create a complete protein when eaten together), and native fields were densely planted to keep down weeds and hold water in the soil. Producing a surplus would support trading and alliance building.

In his book *The Potomac*, Frederick Gutheim noted that the region's first European farmers established a "pioneer corn culture, taken over almost intact from the Indians by the first settlers." To clear fields, trees were killed by girdling, the planting of corn in hills, cultivating it with wooden implements and harvesting and processing the crop with husking bees and mortar and pestle grinding.

Indian corn helped early European settlers survive and established trade with tribes. Europeans first traded copper and other "English trifles" for corn since they were unable to feed themselves, but they were seeking silver, gold and pelts—whatever could be shipped to England and sold. That trade mentality would lead settlers to eventually favor cash crops, like tobacco.

Corn was a fundamental American crop, as Helen Zoe Veit pointed out in *Food in the Civil War Era: The South.* It was first gathered by native people as a wild grain and then selectively bred into a cultivated crop that was larger and had more kernels. Natives used corn in bread, hominy and succotash, and it kept early settlers alive, adapted to English recipes like puddings and breads. Corn was a flexible crop; it could be eaten as a vegetable, dried and ground into grain, fed to livestock or transformed into alcohol. It was fed to enslaved laborers who then picked cotton to be sold, a process that, as Veit pointed out, turned "provender into profit."

Cooking, like food gathering and growing, was based on seasonal needs and resources. When food was abundant, the work would be to preserve it, such as smoked fish or pemmican—a kind of ancient power bar made of

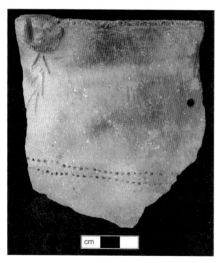 

Left: Archaeological findings at the Shepard and Hughes sites along the Potomac River near Poolesville have included stone and ceramic tools for hunting and cooking. Pot sherds are often marked with incised decorations. *Courtesy Maryland Archaeological Conservation Lab, Jefferson Patterson Park and Museum.*

Right: The Shepard and Hughes sites are classified as Late Woodland villages, and food remnants found mostly at the Hughes site include animal bones, mussel shells, maize, beans, fruit and grain seeds and even this bit of prehistoric berry. *Courtesy Maryland Archaeological Conservation Lab, Jefferson Patterson Park and Museum.*

dried meat and berries bound by fat. Produce stored in earthen caches would be called on in winter—a technique later used by White and Black farmers to preserve a winter stash. Vegetables were also dried, including dried green beans that would become the Appalachian food "leather britches."

Boiling pots are among the archaeological objects used for stone boiling. Stones heated in the fire would be placed in the pot of ingredients to heat and cook them. Those pots likely contained the Indian triad: squash, beans and corn. Meat and fish would be spitted and grilled over flame or cooked in pit ovens—holes, lined with stones, heated with fire and covered with earth.

This was more than survival fare; scented with sweet sunflower oil or animal fat, maple syrup, honey, sumac, pine and juniper—flavors used in other food cultures—they were dishes that were absorbed into American culture. Succotash made with corn, squash and beans eventually evolved into Brunswick stew. The menu included baked beans, clambakes, fish cakes and hominy, baked squash and pumpkin with breads made of corn, chestnut or sweet potato.

Europeans who came to the region, canvassing it for resources and trade potential, found native communities that had adapted and thrived for thousands of years—fifteen thousand years according to archaeological evidence along the Potomac. Two different understandings of land and its use would begin in the mid-1600s, with the dispersion and assimilation of native communities by settlers who staked claims to land and cleared forests.

Historian Stephen Potter noted that the English didn't seem like a threat to native sovereignty—they couldn't feed themselves, and they had no women and no community. In a possibly apocryphal story, a Powhatan chief is recorded as saying to Governor Calvert in 1634, "I will neither bid you go nor stay." The Europeans would, of course, stay. Their moves to Christianize indigenous people and mark territory made the threat evident.

Potter also noted that English settlers exploited the native groups' social and physical borders, allying with one group or another to gain territory and control over other western settlers, including French, Dutch and Swedes. From Boyd's point of view, this shift of sovereignty was natural and hardly worth commenting on: "The Indians lived in the greatest harmony with the settlers, they hunted together for deer and turkeys, while the women and children became domesticated in the families of the English."

As settlers in the Potomac region established communities, the loss of native land and self-government meant that by the early 1700s, most Nanticoke and Piscataway people had left Maryland for Pennsylvania and were later exiled from Pennsylvania after the French and Indian War (1754–63). Many

> Pumpkin. Native Americans boiled, roasted, baked and dried pumpkins, which were new to European settlers. With their thick shell and solid flesh, pumpkins store through the winter. Elizabeth Ellicott Lea wrote, "If you put ripe pumpkins that have not been frosted; in a dry place, they will keep to make puddings till spring." Early recipes call for them baked, fried, mashed, roasted and stewed—in both sweet and savory dishes.

joined a tribal confederation in Ohio territory, but when defeated in the Battle of Fallen Timbers (1794), they fled north to Canada or became part of the Lenape and Iroquois groups.

Eastern tribes were further dispersed as a result of the War of 1812. As the United States expanded and became an organized military power, more than two hundred treaties broke tribal alliances. By the 1820 census, the White population had spread with considerable concentration along the Eastern Seaboard, in cities and following river routes, pushing out native populations.

A mortal blow came with Andrew Jackson's 1830 Indian Removal Act, aimed at the powerful southern tribes of Cherokee and Creeks, which had "stubbornly opposed the progress of population." The act severed their connection to land, history and culture. In the Potomac region, the Nanticokes, Piscataways and Powhatans who remained lived in small communities that were restricted by race laws. They still farmed, hunted and fished, but old ways were lost.

While native groups had borders and territories, their use of the land was different than the first European settlers. Indian groups moved seasonally without a tradition of deeded landownership. By contrast, settlers established land grants and marked boundaries on maps so that land could be sold and inherited.

That land was not valued for ongoing survival but instead for trade goods that could be extracted from it—searching for gold and silver, harvesting animal pelts and growing the cash crop of tobacco on estates, worked by enslaved labor. Later histories would recount the stone, minerals and metals that could be extracted; the water that could power mills and create transportation routes; and the soils that could support livestock and crops. In Montgomery County, Indian trails became major transportation routes, and its many stream valleys would become the sites for mills that ground wheat, barley and lime—products that became mainstays of the local economy.

Explorer Henry Fleet ventured into the Potomac River Valley to Little Falls and in 1627 reported what he found to London merchants in an attempt to pique their interest in trade: "This place without all question is the most pleasant and healthful place in all this country and most convenient for habitation, the air temperate in the summer and not violent in the winter. It abounds in all manner of fish. The Indians in one night will catch thirty sturgeons…and as for deer, buffalo, bears, turkeys, the woods do swarm with them and the soil is exceedingly fertile."

English settlement of the area that would become Montgomery County began years later in 1650 by Robert Brooke, who, Boyd noted, "founded a Protestant settlement of forty persons including his wife and ten children, at Della Brooke on the Patuxent River." His descendant Roger Brooke Farquhar described the landscape at that time as primeval forest teeming with wildlife, streams filled with fish: "All were largely undisturbed by the natives who were unable to make effective warfare against these denizens of the forests and the streams with such primitive weapons as they possessed." One might also say the native people were able to live and thrive in balance with the local environment, even when trading with neighboring tribes.

Brooke does recognize that due to "thriving villages and thickly settled suburban areas, the accelerated destruction of the birds and animals began and has continued to the present time." Some of that particular game included ruffed grouse, wild turkeys, passenger pigeons, woodcocks and bobwhites; "in former days a good fisherman could catch a nice supply of eel, catfish, sunfish, suckers, and perch in the several small streams; and the whitefish or

LOAF SUGAR. Until the late nineteenth century, refined sugar was formed into loaves—really, cone shapes formed in earthenware or iron molds. The boiled cane syrup would be poured into a mold where any non-crystalline matter would drain through a small hole in the tip into a catch pot. White clay would be added, which would absorb remaining molasses, leaving a white loaf, which was dried, trimmed and wrapped. You can imagine why the peaky profile of Sugarloaf Mountain reminded explorers of sugar loaves set in a pantry.

fallfish was gamey fish formerly plentiful." The woods also supplied fox and chicken grapes and wild persimmons, "its pink fruit becoming edible only 'after frost.'" Attentive foragers can still find persimmons, as well as pawpaws, in county forests.

The new world was, for those with means, a land of opportunity—in their eyes a ready source of wealth. In 1712, Christoph von Graffenried, 1st Baron of Bernberg, traveled from his native Switzerland to North Carolina, where he founded the community of New Bern. His explorations of the new country led him to the Shenandoah in hopes of finding a source of silver ore. Instead, he found a landmark: the isolated outcropping that stands out among the rolling Piedmont hills "on our return, we ascended a high mountain standing alone in the midst of a vast flat stretch of country, called Sugar Loaf which means in French Pain de sucre."

This monadnock is a landmark. It is described by John Thomas Scharf in *History of Western Maryland* as "the triple crown of white sandstone of the Sugar-Loaf Mountain stand out as if sculptured monumental objects in the midst of the soft-toned landscape." At the mountain's foot, the water, soil and timber attracted European settlers. More would follow, and as Boyd wrote, new settlers "reduced the land to cultivation....Tobacco and corn were the principal articles cultivated. Great attention was paid to fruit—while the waters of the bay and rivers furnished the greatest delicacies, oysters, wild ducks, and fish. The people were planters and farmers and there was no influence to draw the people together, like in towns and cities, but left the people free to lay the foundation of that peculiar domestic life which has always been the characteristic and charm of Maryland."

The original land grant covering Montgomery County stretched from today's St. Mary's County to Frederick, and as a commercial endeavor, it was divided and subdivided into farms and grants, creating the landscape Boyd described. The names of some of those grants are evocative of relationships and community, some positive (Bradford's Rest, Two Brothers, Younger Brother, Girl's Portion and New Year's Gift) and others less so (Dispute, Gitting's Hah! Hah!!, Bite the Biter, If No Thieves and Trouble Enough Indeed). Some also reflect how the land would be used and hopes for its productivity (Pork Plenty, Turkey Thicket, Goose Pond, Peach Tree Hill, Cow Pasture and Spring Garden).

T.H.S. Boyd wrote that early settlers wasted no time establishing orchards and relying on what they could grow: "[T]he life of a frontiersman, drank their cider and sack, in lieu of coffee and tea, which were seldom used. Apples and peaches were raised in great abundance; two or three varieties

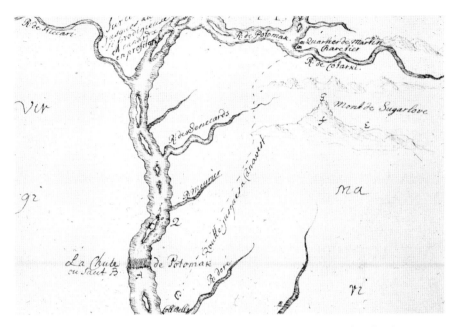

Baron von Graffenried founded the community of New Bern in North Carolina but ventured north in search of raw materials, including metal ore, for trading. His notes include a map of Sugarloaf Mountain. *Courtesy Montgomery History.*

of white apples were cultivated for summer use, while the long stem, red, red streak, and black red streak were the principal varieties for use in autumn and winter."

Roger Brooke Farquhar painted a picture of industrious settlers establishing themselves on this land: "The first settlers were familiar with the rifle and the plow, and the sickle....As settlements progressed, forests were felled and crude log cabins were built by the settler with the aid of his hardy wife. There were times when feasting, frolicking and fox hunting produced diversion. The first crops were tobacco, often grown in a small clearing in the forest; and this continued to be the main crop of the settlers for nearly a century."

The area that would become Montgomery County is along the fall line of the Potomac, where the river drops hundreds of feet and becomes less navigable. It's also at a cultural fall line, between the planter communities of the lower Potomac and the more modest farmsteads of the upper Potomac.

Boyd described planter culture in his review of the county's history: "First, were the old Tobacco Planter, with their baronial estates and armies of slaves. They felled native forests, and planted the virgin soil in tobacco and Indian corn. This did very well so long as there was timber for the axe, and new land for the hoe; and these old lords of manors were happy; they feasted, and frolicked and fox hunted, and made the most of life; those days are known as 'the good old times.'"

Likewise, planter life is described in *History of Western Maryland* as communities of comfortable homes built from the brick used as ballast in English ships, whose residents "dispensed a generous and often courtly hospitality. The table always contained an abundance of food, and the style of living was liberal, not to say prodigal."

It was this prodigal table that gave Maryland cooking a reputation for abundance and generosity, one that would later be made famous and exported by restaurants like Montgomery County's Olney Inn, which opened in 1926 in the former Granville Farquhar farm, where the Inn grew most of its own produce, raised chickens and eggs and smoked its own hams. Cherry Grove was a farm that operated for a few years after 1928 as a colonial-themed country restaurant, offering a blazing fire in the winter and a cool spot under the trees in the summer. A 1929 dinner party menu for Rhode Island senator Peter Goelet Gerry included two roast turkeys, two baked, home-cured Maryland hams "and all the concomitants of a bountiful feast." Dishes like beaten biscuits, Maryland fried chicken and Chesapeake seafood and game called on southern traditions developed by the expertise of enslaved cooks.

Farther up the Potomac, closer to Frederick, German settlements of small farmsteads brought different ways of living and different foods. In *The Potomac*, Gutheim described "the German housewife especially was noted for her skill in preparing butter and cheese, and for her industry and deftness in weaving and knitting. Apple and cherry orchards were to be found on nearly every farm, and the cellar was generally well-stocked with excellent home-brewed beer and cider."

A Guide to the Old Line State, published in 1940 as part of the Federal Writers' Project of the Works Progress Administration, captured the county's two culinary cultures when it describes Maryland cookery as "predominantly Southern" but noted that "[n]evertheless it is the custom to serve sauerkraut with roast turkey, goose, duck, or chicken."

A successful farm operated as a small business, with an attentive eye to the market, stewardship of the land and each family member with assigned jobs. In 1790, Brooke Grove, as described in *Old Homes and History*, covered 14,700 acres and was set up by Roger Brooke V as an "integrated" project:

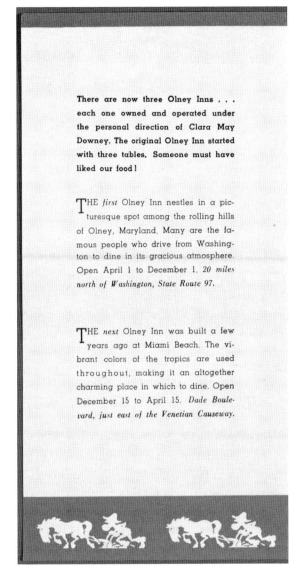

There are now three Olney Inns . . . each one owned and operated under the personal direction of Clara May Downey. The original Olney Inn started with three tables. Someone must have liked our food!

THE *first* Olney Inn nestles in a picturesque spot among the rolling hills of Olney, Maryland. Many are the famous people who drive from Washington to dine in its gracious atmosphere. Open April 1 to December 1. *20 miles north of Washington, State Route 97.*

THE *next* Olney Inn was built a few years ago at Miami Beach. The vibrant colors of the tropics are used throughout, making it an altogether charming place in which to dine. Open December 15 to April 15. *Dade Boulevard, just east of the Venetian Causeway.*

Maryland's Way: The Hammond-Harwood House Cookbook is a collection of Maryland recipes like Liza's Waffles and Genie's Smothered Chicken, which is described as "a very old receipt, long used at the Olney Inn." The skills of these anonymous cooks made Clara Mae Downey's Olney Inn so famous that she opened branches in New York and Miami. *Courtesy New York Public Library.*

stables, barns, blacksmith, carpenter and machine shops, icehouse, meat house, gristmill, sawmill, cider mill and water power. The author, Brooke, takes pains to point out that his ancestor's operation included tenant houses, rather than simpler quarters, and that he never owned a slave. It was recalled that Brooke V used to walk his land and in various corners and spots push in a hole with his cane and drop in a black walnut, eventually creating a valuable harvest for the following generations.

Culinary historian Michael Twitty called these farms a "rural machine," with each family member taking his or her part in production. Men were in the fields, hunting and fishing. Women worked in the house, with only the most rudimentary machines or with the help of slaves or indentured servants. He points out that each season had its tasks, and in the 1920s, Martha Sprigg Poole recalled the work on her grandparents' farm. In the spring, soil in the fields was loosened and weeds turned under to prepare for planting corn, five kernels to each hill—"one for the cut-worm, one for the crow, one to rot and two to grow." June was for haymaking, and by September, the corn was ready to be cut for animal feed and ground into meal. There was always work to be done: tending the family garden, fertilizing fields, storing ice, milking cows, caring for livestock, repairing fences, replenishing the woodpile and general maintenance.

Brooke Grove's operation was unusual. Most of the county's eighteenth-century farmhouses were simple constructions—single-story wooden cabins with sloped roofs that extended to cover a narrow porch. Some had sleeping lofts and perhaps a separate summer kitchen or an ell for storage. Farms were small industrial complexes. Barns would house livestock and their feed, tobacco houses were for drying and curing leaves and a stone springhouse would be used to store and cool food and dairy products. Some farmsteads would have a smokehouse or distillery.

Near Muncaster Mill, King's Distillery produced whiskey in the late 1800s, when Maryland became known for its rye whiskey. The King family also distilled lesser-valued corn whiskey, advertised as "for the help, at harvest time."

All was not sober and sensible farm life. Josiah Henson described the habits of the "dissipated planters of the neighborhood" and of his master, Isaac Riley. They would meet at taverns to drink whiskey, brandy and water and to gamble, which led to fights where "glasses were thrown, dirks drawn, and pistols fired," to the point that they couldn't find their ways home and "each one ordered a slave, a particular attendant to come after him and help him home." Henson hauled his master home "with the ease with which I would handle a bag of corn."

Mrs. Frances Trollope in her 1830 book *Domestic Manners of Americans* described a visit to a farm near what is now Avenel, where she judged the husband to be idle, "preferring hunting (as they call shooting) to any other occupation. The consequence was that but a very portion of the dividend [the wife's dowry land] was cultivated, and their poverty was extreme."

At another farm, she found a "worthless father" who drank whiskey and "would not suffer them to raise, even by their own labor, any garden vegetables, and they lived upon their fat pork, salt fish and cornbread, summer and winter, without variation."

She commented, "The luxury of whiskey is more appreciated by the men than all the green delicacies from the garden, and if all the ready money goes for that and their darling chewing tobacco, none can be spent by the wife for garden seeds."

Nevertheless, taverns were waystations for travelers and community gathering places, post offices and trading places. Charles Hungerford rented his tavern, which was built of hand-hewn logs and had an eight-foot-wide fireplace, from its owner, Joseph Willson. In his journals, George Washington recorded finishing his business in "George Town" and "[b]reakfasted in a small village called Williamsburg in which stands the Ct. House of Montgomery County." Rockville was called Williamsburg at that time, and although George Washington didn't sleep there, he did dine there.

Hungerford's tavern also served as a meeting place for the county seat and for a time gave its name to the community that grew up around it, later to become Rockville. This tavern was a polling place for elections during the Revolution and the site of a notable vote in June 1774 on a resolution to break off trade with Great Britain in support of the blockaded port of Boston.

Crossroads taverns were places of personal, political and economic connections that linked individual farms to a wider community. Before 1779, the court sat in the tavern Leonard Davis had taken over from Hungerford. Scholl's Tavern in Clarksburg was the site of political party meetings, including for the Federalists in 1811.

On Barnesville Road, the Mary Morningstar House dates back to the original 1743 log cabin with a later two-story frame addition in 1824. Local lore and shared family memories recall that the log cabin was used as a tavern and later as a small confectionery and grocery. The cabin's main room, now used as a living room, is much larger than standard for a family common room, and steps in the corner curve up to what was four rooms—likely for travelers. As the current owners work in their garden, they regularly unearth remnants that offer clues to the life of the house, including shards of blue willow china, rusted fittings for horse bridles and wagons and even a drinking cup.

While crossroads attracted taverns, the county's streams and waterways offered mill sites. Today, the streams seem invisible, hidden in culverts or buffered from development in county and state parks, but they were the original sites of local industry. There were at one time at least fourteen

At the time of this postcard, circa 1916, Hungerford's Tavern was a scenic landmark, described as "where was passed one of the first resolutions against Great Britain, which brought on the 'Boston Tea Party.' In 1776 the First Court for Montgomery County was held here. Where Washington, Braddock and Lafayette entertained. Rockville, Md." *Courtesy Montgomery History.*

The owners of a circa 1743 house on Barnesville Road have found shards and artifacts when digging in their garden, including pieces of horse tack and an aged drinking cup. Speculation is that the house was a tavern and later a shop. Its common room is far larger than a family parlor, and in a corner next to the fireplace, narrow stairs lead upstairs, which was divided into four rooms. *Courtesy George Kousoulas.*

water-powered mills along Rock Creek and as many as forty mills in the county circa 1800.

If well sited, water was an efficient power source. The stream had to have a steady flow, with topography that could accommodate a millpond and millrace. The stream's water was backed up behind a dam to create a millpond, which fed the wheel via a culvert called the millrace, turning a bladed wheel using the force of the water and gravity, which drove connected milling, grinding or sawing machinery.

The mill also had to be near the farms that would supply raw material and have access to markets where goods could be sold. A 1790 advertisement describes a promising candidate: "For sale. A Valuable Mill-seat with about 217 acres of land situated on the mouth of Seneca Creek and the boat navigation of Potowmack…it is a capital seat for a Merchant-mill the stream strong and constant in an extensive neighbourhood well adapted to wheat, and no Mill prepared for Merchant work within many miles."

As Michael Dwyer noted in *Montgomery County Mills*, mill sites were made useful beyond the grain season by being paired with a sawmill. The addition

When this picturesque view of Muncaster Mill was taken, the mill was likely an artifact, replaced by more powerful steam-driven mills. *Courtesy Montgomery History, photograph by Lewis Reed.*

"Intoxicating Liquor" in Montgomery County
"[T]he punishment of drunkenness as a crime wrought a revolution in some localities which was highly beneficial to material interests of the province."

—*The History of Western Maryland*, 1882

Josiah Henson recalled in his autobiography how the drunkenness of his owners changed his life more than once. First, it was the death of his first owner, the "jovial" Dr. McP. "The doctor was riding from one of his scenes of riotous excess, when, falling from his horse, crossing a little run, not a foot deep, he was unable to save himself from drowning." Henson's family was sold and scattered. His second owner, R., was "coarse and vulgar in his habits," and Henson recorded his entertainments as gambling, running horses, fighting gamecocks and drinking whiskey and brandy and water "all day long." Quarrels were inevitable, but one of these fights didn't end; Henson was ambushed and badly beaten, leaving him "unable to raise my hands to my head from that day to this."

Maryland's English settlers sought to re-create an aristocratic life on their land grant estates, leaving the labor to enslaved workers and relying on tobacco as a cash crop. Social life, including hunts, called for plenty of alcohol. Among the early settlers were Scotch and Irish who carried on their grain distilling traditions, using rye and eventually corn. Irish workers were contracted to build a railroad at the base of Sugarloaf Mountain, and in his *History of Montgomery County*, T.H.S. Boyd wrote, "A car containing tools and provisions with 'gigger' cups and big jugs, was dispatched from each terminus of the road to clean off snow, and when the two parties met on the road double giggers were dealt out by the 'grog boss,' and great hilarity pleasantly followed, unless the laborers happened to be hostile, and then an attempt might be made to repeat the battle of the Boyne." Irish workers on the Great Falls canal were given three gills of rum a day, and once operating, the canal acquired a reputation for "roudies." Lockkeepers sold alcohol to passing boatmen, leading the company to enact rules limiting the sales. Much later, during Prohibition, the no-longer-operating canal would become a landing place for bootleggers.

Drinking in the county sounds like a free-for-all, but it wasn't without oversight, from its early establishment. In *Old Homes and History*, Roger Brooke Farquhar noted that around the 1770s, "county business settled into a comfortable routine." Governance included "adjusting tavern rates. Among the latter were such items as a hot diet for gentlemen, with a pint of beer or cider, three shillings; the same fare for a gentleman's servant, two shillings and sixpence...whiskey, five shillings per quart; and peach brandy, eight shillings per quart."

While alcohol could enliven socializing and motivate work, it was also seen as a moral, safety and economic problem by a growing temperance movement in the United States. Governments also realized that whiskey taxes could be a significant source of public revenue. In Montgomery County in 1833, well before the 1893 establishment of the Anti-Saloon League, the trustees of the Brookeville Academy "secured the passage of a law prohibiting the sale of intoxicating liquors in the town of Brookeville or its vicinity," and the county's first temperance society was organized in Rockville. The county's Methodist churches supported the local option, whereby local communities could prohibit alcohol sales, but it became a political issue, splitting party tickets. In 1880, a special election made Montgomery a dry county.

Between 1880 and 1933, overlapping with national Prohibition, alcohol sales were prohibited in the county. And like the rest of the country, Montgomery kept drinking. Alcohol was a value-added product that could be more easily brought to market than the raw grain. In 1878, Montevideo was sold to Joseph Dyson, who never lived there but rented it to tenant farmers, including Bill Gunnell, who made bootleg "Montevideo whiskey."

Every community establishes laws and licenses for selling and serving liquor, and "control states" hold the authority to purchase and distribute liquor. Montgomery is one of the few U.S. counties that has control rights and conducts the wholesale distribution of liquor. In 1933, the county established its Liquor Control Board to oversee liquor regulation. In 1951, the Department of Liquor Control was created to manage distribution to licensed outlets and to county liquor stores. Over time, the number of county liquor stores has grown from seven to twenty-five stores, and revenue has grown as well.

The Department of Liquor Control is self-supporting through its revenues, and per a 2015 League of Women Voters report, it returns about $25 million each year to the County's General Fund. County government points out that these funds help support public service providers like firefighters, teachers and police.

Nonetheless, there are regular calls for this unique system to end. Some believe that the government shouldn't be in the liquor business, others that customer service would improve in a privatized system. Restaurateurs complain of added bureaucracy, missed deliveries and poor selection. A 1980 study found favoritism and conflicts of interest in hiring and purchasing. The system has hindered local craft beer brewing and vineyards, especially in the Agricultural Reserve, where farmers seek to create value-added businesses. In 2014, craft brewers were allowed to bypass county oversight, and eventually special orders were privatized, allowing producers to sell directly to restaurants.

This patchwork of private and public distribution returns significant revenues, but a patchwork is never easy to navigate—perhaps that's the idea.

of a blacksmith, wheelwright, tannery and cooper shops created a kind of eighteenth- or nineteenth-century tech center. Mills saved hours of farm labor, diversified the agricultural economy and created value-added goods, which gained a higher market price. Flaxseed was ground for oil, lime for plaster and animal bone for fertilizer. Sawmills turned logs into lumber.

Gristmills ground corn and wheat. Country custom mills took a toll, a percentage of the meal or flour, while merchant mills purchased grain from farmers, ground it and sold it. An early mill on the Hawlings River, north of Brookville, also supplied ship's biscuit to vessels sailing out of Joppa and Bladensburg.

In 1828, Robertson's Mill (later Muncaster's Mill) advertised its services: "We are making preparation to receive crops of wheat from the farmers, to be manufactured, and I think we will be safe in saying our flour, if the wheat is clean and good, will do us credit in any market."

Gristmills in all sections of the county did a lively business into the early 1900s, custom grinding wheat into flour for the farmers' own use or for local sales. In *The Potomac Adventure*, Ann Paterson Harris recorded that Lucy J. Pumphrey operated the "Glen Roller Mills," listing her as "Manufacturer

In this photo, taken at some point after 1932 for the Historic American Buildings Survey, the man posing next to the derelict Muncaster Mill water wheel gives a sense of its size and potential power. *Courtesy Library of Congress.*

The Bowman brothers' steam-powered gristmill, in Germantown, was established in 1895. After a fire in 1914, it was rebuilt as the Liberty Mill, and in 1918, it was operated by three brothers, Charles, Eldridge and William Upton. It advertised a capacity of two hundred barrels per day and was operated into the 1940s. *Courtesy Montgomery History.*

and Dealer in The Celebrated 'White Daisy' Patent and Consolation Flours, Best Stone Ground Corn Meal for Family Use." She also offered "Pure Ground Rye, Corn, and Oats for Feed, Sawed Stove Wood, etc."

Fulling mills turned wool into fabric, saving home labor by carding, cleaning and dyeing, as well as "fulling" wool into blankets and fabric. Fulling removed grease and compacted the fibers by washing and pounding the fabric using water-powered hammers and fuller's earth (an absorbent clay).

Many mills were established to supply the revolutionary army with "woolen, cotton, linsey, bedtick, chequer, etc." In 1790s Brookeville, Thomas' Mill took grain, and so as not to compete, Newlin's Mill, at the west end of town, instead did flax, castor and clover seed for oil. The embargo on British imports during the War of 1812 expanded the market for local cloth, and the Brookeville Woolen Factory was established to make fabric for "clothes for servants," which meant slaves.

The county's water-powered mills began to decline in the late 1800s, replaced by steam, gasoline and electric turbines, and few local mills operated after 1925. The demand for local grain, beef and cloth also declined, as the Midwest farms and mills, connected by rail to East Coast markets, could grow and process at a larger, more efficient scale. In 1922, the WSSC bought Burnt Mill on the Northwest Branch, a gristmill that had operated since 1745. It would use the site for a water filtration plant to serve expanding suburban communities. Most of the county's mills were gone by the 1930s, abandoned, subsumed by road construction or dismantled for their materials. Many of the county's farmers would shift from grain to dairy, produce and eggs for the local market.

As Dwyer noted, writing about Pyle's Mill at Ten Mile Creek and Old Baltimore Road, "it is difficult to believe that this was once the location of an elaborate enterprise built along a supposedly busy road, which linked the wheat-growing interior of the state with the grain port of Baltimore." He could have been writing about any of the mills, which live on primarily in road and place names: Veirs Mill, Muncaster Mill, Jones Mill, Plyers Mill, Kemp's Mill, Glen Mill, Bell's Mill and Dufief Mill.

Local milling made Montgomery independent of the mills in Georgetown, but both raw materials and finished goods went down the rolling roads to the port of Georgetown, connecting the county to wider markets and world events.

After petitioning the Maryland General Assembly to establish a town on the Potomac, "above the mouth of Rock Creek, adjacent to the Inspection House," in what was then Frederick County, sixty acres of land for

Georgetown was purchased in 1751. In 1787, it was incorporated as a city, but it was soon ceded to the District of Columbia in 1791. Nonetheless, it remained a political entity until 1895, when Congress ended its status as an independent city.

With that decision, Montgomery County lost land but gained the federal city as a neighbor, which contributed to the county's prosperity. The new capital required marking on a map, which created work in surveying, land deeds and speculation. As the city grew, there was construction, road building and stone cutting; with an increasing population came a market for crops and commerce.

Georgetown was just below where the Potomac was no longer navigable, making it the first spot to collect goods from upriver farms in Maryland and Virginia. For a time, it rivaled Baltimore, and its customhouse collected considerable duties on goods from London and Amsterdam. Amid today's condominiums and boutiques are remnants of Georgetown's industrial past—mills and warehouses hard-by the river and the C&O Canal, with wealthy estates on the high ground, away from the noise and smell of a working waterfront.

Robert Peter, some of whose holdings would later become Montevideo in Montgomery County, had a tea shipment arrive in August 1774—not a popular product with colonists. It wasn't dumped as in Boston or set on fire as in Annapolis, but he was called to account by his fellow residents. The matter was turned over to a committee, whose members judged that the tea should be placed in storage until further notice—likely until the furor had passed.

As has ever been the case in Washington, wars change the city and its environs. Mustering armies and the new residents to manage the conflicts require provisioning. In 1776, Michael Cockendorfer set up a tavern on the Georgetown-Frederick Road near today's Chevy Chase. Newport Mills was established in 1774 by Thomas Johns and Thomas Richardson to sell grain to the army.

Food provisions were a logistical challenge. In 1778, an agent was appointed and instructed to set up stores of wheat and flour in Georgetown, with care not to let the purchased meat spoil. A 1779 act required each county to ready an immediate supply of flour and other provisions, with a commissioner appointed to collect wheat, flour, rye and corn. The stores also included salt to preserve shad and herring from Potomac fisheries, located mostly above Little Falls. General Washington's "assistant commissary, Thomas Beall, scoured Montgomery County for whiskey and cider brandy."

The county was also a source for hay and forage for horses and the oxen to transport salt beef and pork, as well as cattle on the hoof. Because Montgomery was not grazing country, though, cattle were scarce. All this provisioning was somewhat slowed by farmers' skepticism of the new money issued by the State of Maryland.

During the Civil War, Georgetown was again an important provisioning center. It was a port and landing place for canalboats, which were an important supply route and a constant target of Confederate forces. Its flour mills and warehouses were valuable resources. Union troops were billeted on the Georgetown University campus, Tudor Place housed Union officers and banks, churches and schools were turned into hospitals that would shudder under a wave of wounded after nearby battles.

Tudor Place, on the high ground of Georgetown, was built in 1805 by Thomas Peter and his wife, Martha Parke Custis Peter, a granddaughter of Martha Washington. Their daughter, Britannia Peter, was born there

Georgetown was originally part of Montgomery County and served as a port connection for county farmers and merchants, connected by the C&O Canal to the Ohio Valley and by the Potomac River to Alexandria and then to Baltimore. *Courtesy Montgomery History.*

in 1815, could recall Lafayette's visit to the house in 1824, saw the house through the Civil War and died there in 1911. She was instrumental in preserving the house along with family artifacts and papers.

During much of her life, Tudor Place was provisioned by Oaklands, the family farm at Seneca Creek in Montgomery County. Many city families relied on country farms for food as well as income. Among other things, Britannia's *Reminiscences* describe what and how they ate:

> *There were twenty hogs brought down from "Oakland" every fall and put up in the meat house here. There were hams, middlings, jowl, spare-ribs, cherries, the little griskins, sausage and lard. That was pork worth eating, not such as we by [sic] now, which is pickled! Everything was fried with pork in those days and a delicious flavor it gave to things too.*
>
> *The hogs were cut up, salted and packed in barrels for six weeks, after which they were hung up with white oak splits in the meat house and smoked. Poor old Will Johnson went to start his fire in the smokehouse and keep it smoking but he never let the fire burn up to heat the meat kept it smothered and smoking continually.*
>
> *Of course, there were more than twenty hogs raised at the farms! There were the negroes to be fed. Pork and corn meal were the principal articles of food for them. Besides, there were always hogs sent to market and sold.*
>
> *I often think now how different it all is from what it was in those good old days. Then, people lived for the most part within themselves! They raised their own beef, mutton, hogs, poultry and fine fowles we had. We had our own dairy where the butter was made. Then, there was the garden where the vegetables were raised the orchard, from which we had an abundance of fine fruit. The fruit was put up for winter use, either preserved canned or dried; vegetables were stored away and herbs were dried for seasoning. And where was there a place in those days without its herb garden!*

Georgetown's industry and port, and the money they generated, earned the city political power; it became "a major voice in the Montgomery County delegation in Annapolis." Obviously, Georgetown's power shifted when the city was ceded to the District and again when Congress ended its governance as an independent jurisdiction. In Montgomery County, political power would for many years rest with the rural communities that were the source of its wealth but shift again as down-county communities developed, contributed taxes and jobs and grew in population after World Wars I and II.

By the luck of its location next the nation's capital city, Montgomery County was on a prosperous path. By 1873, the Metropolitan Branch Railroad ran diagonally through the county from northwest to southeast, putting nearly every neighborhood within easy reach. When T.H.S. Boyd lauded this progress, he seemed to be describing the tension between a cottage suburban rural lifestyle and actual rural production that we face today:

> *As the location of Washington seems to be on the ground prepared for a site of the seat of Government of a great Nation, so Montgomery County seems prepared to furnish supplies of all kinds for the inhabitants of such a city; Milk, Butter, Poultry, Hay, Fruit, and Vegetables, in fact, everything which will not stand long carriage. Also, by means of this road, to furnish locations for country residences for those who can afford it, the whole line from Washington to Sugar Loaf Mountain furnishes sites for cottages, where abundant water of the best quality, shade, trees and soil most favorable for gardeners can be found.*

Sophisticated Native American Flavors—Trout with Sumac

Contrary to popular understanding, Native American foods across the continent offered a wide variation of flavor based in local ingredients and the local climate. Honed through generations, farming, foraging, cooking and dining skills and traditions reveal sophisticated flavors, and as Sean Sherman pointed out in Sioux Chef, *the Native American pantry is local and seasonal, with no processed foods, sugar, dairy or wheat—a healthy way to eat.*

According to Native American chef Nico Albert, this recipe traveled with her Cherokee ancestors across the country. Trout and wild sumac are available nearly everywhere across the continent, including the lands along the Potomac and in the county's many streams. It is a simple recipe that you can make as complicated as you like by catching your own trout or foraging your own sumac. In North America, the staghorn sumac was used for its bright, citrus flavor in drinks and foods and as medicine. "Indian lemonade" is easy to make by simply soaking the berries and then sweetening the rosy red drink. Sumac's bright-red berries are easy to distinguish from the white berries of poison sumac.

1 whole trout fillet (boned and gutted)
Salt and pepper
Ground sumac
Sunflower oil (any high-heat tolerant oil can be used,
such as canola, corn or vegetable oil)

A 12-inch cast-iron skillet is the best tool to get nice crispy skin on this trout, but any skillet or flat-bottomed pan that can withstand high heat will work just fine. Place your skillet over high heat. While the skillet is heating, pat the trout dry on both sides. Season both sides liberally with salt, pepper and sumac. Drizzle both sides of the fish with oil.

When the skillet is just beginning to smoke, place the fish skin-side down in the pan, lightly pressing with a spatula to ensure that the skin has good contact with the pan. Cook for 3 to 4 minutes until the skin is crisp and then flip the fish over and cook the flesh for about 2 more minutes to cook through. Remove the fish to a plate for serving.

Albert suggests serving this dish with sautéed wild greens and mushrooms—another dish that will hone your foraging skills.

Chapter 3

LIFE ALONG THE CANAL

Today, a walk along Montgomery County's stretch of the C&O Canal towpath can be a quiet contemplation of nature—a sharp eye will spot goldfinches flashing through the trees, an attuned ear will hear the solemn splash of turtles dropping into the water from their sunning logs and in the spring, you may smell the scents of softening earth and flowing water. Along the towpath that weaves through the woods, the whitewashed lockhouses have the blocky simplicity of a child's drawing, and each bend reveals a new view.

But such serenity would be hard to find in the early nineteenth century. The canal was an active commercial route, with braying mules, calls from boat to boat and horns to alert the lockkeeper, water rushing through the locks and boatmen straining to keep the boats steady. At the Seneca Stonecutting Mill, you would hear the sounds of sawing and grinding to cut blocks of pinkish sandstone that would be shipped down the canal and used to build Washington, D.C. Think truck stop or lumberyard.

On its mule-towed boats and in its sandstone lockhouses, the C&O Canal was a place and way of life distinct in the county. The canal struggled through bankruptcies and receiverships, always in competition with the railroad, eventually succumbing to a flood in the 1920s. But through its life, the canal left a legacy of food and foodways that includes Boatman's Bean Soup and what might be the real Maryland fried chicken.

In early America, waterways were natural highways, and the Potomac, with its tributaries reaching into surrounding lands and its broad and protected opening into the Chesapeake Bay, had the potential to be a hub for transportation and thus commerce, settlement and investment. Ports were established at Georgetown and Alexandria, and fords and ferries linked communities in Maryland and Virginia.

The Potomac was a commercial route even for those who weren't operating a legitimate business. T.H.S. Boyd wrote about the people who lived in a settlement called Cooney, the river's Virginia shore near Little Falls, who "obtained from the wrecks a bountiful supply of flour, meat and groceries, and with fish taken from the river, furnished them with their principal means of support."

Waterways were the site of early transportation routes and infrastructure. The water offered a motive force, and there was no need to clear land. In *History of Western Maryland*, Scharf wrote, "A network of fresh limpid streams covers the surface of the county, affording power for milling purposes as well as abundant water for farming and grazing." These streams would become engines of industry and transportation, key to the county's economic success. He wrote, "Nothing more clearly attests the energy and enterprise of a community than the attention bestowed upon roads and bridges, the highways of communication between different portions of the neighborhood and the outside world. It is one of the distinguishing features of general enlightenment."

When Scharf was writing, in 1882, the Metropolitan Branch of the B&O Railroad extended through the county, at first connecting farmers with markets and suppliers in the District and later connecting suburbanites with federal jobs. At that time, the C&O Canal had been open to Cumberland for almost thirty years, hauling coal and farm produce to Georgetown mills. Rough country roads were being paved and were among the highest-cost items in the county's 1881 budget, at more than $13 million. Scharf continued, "It will thus be readily observed that Montgomery possesses unusual facilities for traffic with leading commercial centres."

While early settlers might have viewed the Potomac as a natural highway, it is navigable only to Little Falls, and certainly not at the rocky seventy-six-foot drop at Great Falls, both in lower Montgomery County. Goods would have to be hauled overland—slow and expensive, which drove the move to use the county's streams for milling and to build a canal that could bypass natural obstacles and create a route west to the Ohio Valley's coal and farm produce.

Spurred to compete in trade with England, which held the St. Lawrence, and with Spain, which held the Mississippi, George Washington surveyed

The seventy-six-foot drop at Great Falls makes for dramatic scenery but prevents navigation, which prompted the construction of the C&O Canal. *Courtesy New York Public Library.*

possible routes through the Alleghenies in 1784 and enlisted the support of the state legislatures of Virginia and Maryland.

The project was initially undertaken as a series of bypass canals on the Virginia side of the river, but they were insufficient; between 1770 and 1820, only farmers around White's Ferry were shipping wheat to Georgetown. The Potomac Company was formed to build a single canal from Georgetown to Cumberland, with the expectation that it would continue to Pittsburgh.

When John Quincy Adams broke ground on July 4, 1828, Charles Carroll was doing the same for the Baltimore and Ohio Railroad. Throughout the canal's operation it would compete with the railroad for routes and customers.

The canal was also in competition with roadbuilding. Numerous roads in the county were laid out in 1777, with landowners appointed as overseers, who could be fined for neglect of their duty. The Washington Turnpike Company was incorporated in 1805 and ran along the path of what is now Rockville Pike, from Frederick to Georgetown, connecting farms to the port city. Its tolls were twelve and a half cents for twenty sheep, twenty hogs or for a chair or chaise with one horse and two wheels and twenty-five cents for twenty head of cattle or for a chariot, coach, stage, wagon, phaeton or chaise with two horses and four wheels. In 1849, the Brookeville and Washington Turnpike Company connected Brookeville with Georgetown along what would become Georgia Avenue, with branch routes to Sandy Spring and Ashton.

From its beginning, the company's charter was repeatedly extended as work proceeded slowly and the company incurred debt. Through the canal's construction and operation, companies would be formed and reformed to refinance the project, with different routes and parties vying for advantage. While it was recognized that the canal would add value to the local economy and to abutting lands, the initial costs for infrastructure are always off-putting.

Crews of Irish indentured workers to build the canal were recruited through ads in Dublin, Belfast and Cork newspapers. The pay ranged from eight to twelve dollars per month, and workers were promised meat three times a day, plenty of bread and vegetables and "a reasonable allowance of whiskey."

The warehouse at Edward's Ferry was part of a trade and transportation network that connected farmers, merchants and customers from the Ohio Valley, Virginia, Georgetown and Baltimore. *Courtesy Montgomery History.*

To build the Monocacy Aqueduct, they used stone from the "White Quarry" at the base of Sugarloaf, transported by cog railway on grooved wooden "string-pieces" that carried flatcars with iron wheels pulled by horses or gravity. Sixty men quarried and one hundred cut stones; thirty-three served as masons, ten as carpenters, one as blacksmith and five as a boat crew to transport sand.

The crews were sustained by coarse rations—even on the ship over, their rations were supplied by the canal company. As Elizabeth Kytle noted in *Home on the Canal*, "These people had undoubtedly become all too accustomed to very plain fare at best, and could hardly have been picky eaters. Even so, they often found the daily rations of bread and meat, handed out once a day by overseers, too revolting to choke down."

Local whiskey was also provisioned, and sometimes workers fell into warring camps—the Corkonians and the Longfords, as Boyd recorded. In 1832, the canal company tried prohibition, hoping to regain time and efficiency from their disorderly workforce. Like most prohibitions, it didn't work: "One engineer reported that when the men were denied liquor during the working day they drank at night. In his opinion, the same amount of whiskey that they drank at night, had it been stretched out over the day in nips, would have had but small undesirable effect. Gulped at night, however, by men who must have been tired to the marrow of their bones, it quickly made them either fighting drunk or falling-down drunk. Many a morning found some of them lying where they had dropped in their tracks, unable to do a lick of work."

In *History of Western Maryland*, Scharf recorded the reputation of canal life. At a funeral for local Catholic priest Father John McElroy, two men spoke, held up as "living epistles." They claimed he had delivered them from "the moral corruptions and evil associations of canal life," which all sounds very intriguing. But these were men who were paid to work, not settle a family and make their way. Few women and children were brought over, and along with fights, there were strikes and killing fevers.

By 1829, the canal had reached Offutt's Crossroads—the intersection of River and Falls Roads. It reached Cumberland in 1842 and was opened, with ceremony, for navigation along its full length in October 1850. It began with a procession through the streets of Cumberland, enlivened with bands, crowds and cannon fire. A delegation of dignitaries embarked in a flotilla of five boats that passed through a lock. That passage was celebrated with a "collation prepared by a committee of the canal company." The day ended with a banquet at Barnum's Hotel in Cumberland, where celebrants drank a toast: "The Chesapeake and Ohio Canal and the Baltimore and Ohio Railroad. The former has happily reached its ebony harvests amid the coals fields of the Alleghenies; may the latter journey vigorously on westward until it rejoices amidst the golden plains of the far Californias."

Boats carried agricultural produce—flour, wheat and corn—as well as lime, coal and stone. From its earliest operation, the canal competed with the railroad, which, counterintuitively, raised its rates for hauling flour. When the canal raised its rates, thinking the market could bear the higher price, the railroad dropped its rates and picked up former canal customers.

Like any infrastructure project, the canal made connections that stimulated economic activity. The Goose Creek Canal in Loudoun County reached south to Aldie and could deliver goods across the Potomac to Edward's Ferry. The warehouse there stored grain from surrounding farms that could then be loaded onto canalboats. Eugene Jarboe ran a store there and operated as the postmaster, creating a community gathering place. Hatton Waters owned a canal barge and a warehouse next to the canal near Pennyfield lock, where he also stored and transported grain from nearby farms.

Tolls were charged based on the cargo, weight and mileage. In 1851, whiskey and spirits, fresh and salted fish, slaughtered hogs, bacon and meat paid two cents per ton for the first twenty miles and one cent for every mile after. Flour, oats, cornmeal and pork were shipped downstream, and salted fish, potatoes, salt and oysters were shipped upstream. In 1875, 1 million tons of cargo were shipped via the canal, generating $500,000 in toll revenue.

This stereograph view of Georgetown showing the C&O Canal and Potomac River between 1860 and 1880 is not the quaint neighborhood we know today but rather a scene of infrastructure and commerce. *Courtesy New York Public Library.*

Georgetown had been established as a port and was described in 1818 as "the residence of shopkeepers." By 1851, in Georgetown there were five flour mills, a gristmill, a cotton mill, a soap factory, an iron foundry, two bakeries and a lime kiln. Even the canal's water was a commodity, and the company sold the mills the water they needed to power their operations.

During the Civil War, the canal was a critical supply line for Union troops. As Union colonel Charles P. Stone reported in 1861, "The Canal is absolutely necessary to the well-being of this neighborhood, being one of the best small-grain districts in the State." As such, it also was a target for Confederate troops, and naturally, business suffered. Raids stopped canal operations, and income decreased at the same time repair costs increased. It didn't help that some canal company employees were Southern sympathizers and that others were drafted into the Union army. Toward the end of the war, trade increased; 1870 was a prosperous year, leaving the canal and mills competing for limited water during a drought season, complicated by a flood that washed out culverts.

Canalboats carried 120 tons of cargo. The center cabin included a galley, a tiny stateroom and sleeping bunks, with a mule stable and hay room at the stern. Mules towed the boats; if a boatman could afford two teams, the trip would be quicker and more profitable, and smart boatmen took good care of their mules.

Louisa May Alcott, who nursed in a Georgetown Civil War hospital, observed the community's street life, which included foraging pigs and mules employed to pull boats and wagons. In between duties, she had time to record her observations of their personalities: "The mules were my especial delight.... The coquettish mule had small feet, a nicely trimmed tassel of a tail, perked up ears, and seemed much given to little tosses of the head, affected skips and prances; and, if he wore the bells, or were bedizzened with a bit of finery, put on as many airs as any belle. The moral mule was a stout, hard-working creature, always tugging with all his might; often pulling away after the rest had stopped....I respected this style of mule; and, had I possessed a juicy cabbage, would have pressed it upon him, with thanks for his excellent example."

Along with provisioning the mule team, boatmen had to feed themselves, and food on the boats would change at each leg of the trip. The Mose brothers would load their boat in Cumberland and make their way downstream to Sharpsburg, where their mother would be ready with clean laundry and baked goods for their weeklong trip to Georgetown. They stocked the boat with dried beans, some canned goods and a beer keg of spring water for cooking and drinking. It was a snug ride, shared with mule teams. In *Home on*

Shared with mules and cargo, life on board a canalboat was a "snug ride." Boats carried two mules that could be switched out when one needed a rest. In *Home on the Canal*, J.P. Mose recalled that most people took good care of their mule teams—after all, "without your team, your boat wouldn't go. Just like a car without gasoline. Once you got them going in and out of the boats, you had no trouble. Because they knew where they got their dinner and their breakfast." *Courtesy Montgomery History.*

the Canal, J.P. Mose described the galley: "On the right side of the steps was your stove…a cupboard in the corner, and between the cupboard and where you went down the steps was a little door where you kept your potatoes, your ham if you had ham, like a pantry."

These pantry staples kept the boat crews fed. Mose recalled that bean soup was a specialty of his brother's. He'd also make biscuits and pick up seasonal vegetables like lima beans and corn on the cob purchased from the lockkeeper's gardens. His brother didn't bake, but there were several places along the canal to buy homemade pies like apple, cherry—"mostly pies with crust on top."

His wife, Mary Colbert Mose, grew up boating and recalled that "bean soup was the boatsman's great meal. Bean soup and rivvels made with eggs. Fried chicken. Fish. Coffee. Anything at all. If we wanted to bake, we had our little baker—a regular oven."

Evelyn Pryor Liston also grew up boating but didn't like cooking for her father on the boat, even though she had her dog with her and friends on other boats. All the children looked forward to arriving in Georgetown, where they'd be given a dime to spend at the Candy Kitchen on M Street. They got their first taste of banana splits and mulled the purchase of taffy, licorice, peanuts in the can and cough drops bought in boxes for a Christmas treat. Treats in Georgetown weren't just for children. Mose recalled that after unloading, they'd get themselves a big steak.

Boating life wasn't a cruise. There were constant chores and duties, including putting out hay for the mule teams, greasing their harnesses and cleaning the boat's lamps and reflectors. When Mose and his brother were twelve and thirteen, their father fell ill, so they took over the boat and brought their sister along to cook. Mose considered life on board as "roughing it."

Life in the lockhouses was also a steady round of chores. Lockkeepers were called out at all times of day and night by passing boats, and they were also responsible for maintaining, inspecting and repairing the canal and its locks. The job came with a house, but the pay was low, so lockkeepers became entrepreneurs—selling and buying from passing boats.

Harvey Brant got his coal off the boats and used their corn to fatten his hogs. He sold hot dogs and vegetables and sold bread to the boatmen from Caskey's Bakery in Hagerstown, which he bought for seven cents and sold for ten cents a loaf.

Families often "went boating," which was not the pleasant afternoon it sounds like. Boaters had to care for the boat, the mules, their kit, the cargo and for themselves, and every family member had a job to do. *Courtesy Montgomery History.*

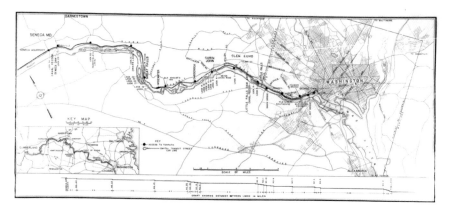

This map marks the lockhouse locations from Washington, D.C., to Seneca. *Courtesy Montgomery History.*

Raymond Riley and Helen Riley Bodmer's father ran Riley's lock, and they recalled some of the food they ate. In *Home on the Canal*, Raymond noted, "The kids every Saturday would come down and we'd take a boat and go out in the river and get wood and bring it in and cut it up and put it in [the fireplace]. We'd have little picnics down there. Boil eggs in an old tea can, fish that they'd caught, or 'stuff you buy out of the store that would have to be cooked, like hot dogs.'"

Helen Riley remembered Allnutt's General Merchandise store, which was just up the road from the lock and has now been renovated by the county as a historic site and operates as the Poole Store. They bought flour and cornmeal from the nearby Tschiffely's Mill. But they never bought bread because their mother baked bread, as well as cakes and pies—"lemon pie, coconut, chocolate and lemon-topped cakes, layer cakes, pancakes for breakfast."

The Rileys kept a meat house at the corner of their River Road property where they smoked and salted meat using a fire built on the dirt floor. They bought beef but raised chickens and hogs. They also planted a big garden, as did most people, with potatoes, radishes, lettuce, carrots, beets, broccoli, cauliflower and turnips. In the fall, they'd dig a big hole, line it with straw, create one big layer of vegetables ("you couldn't pile things on top of each other") and cover it with a big hill of dirt with space for a doorway. This sort of root cellar was used around the county by Black and White farm families.

From Washington, D.C.'s earliest days, the Potomac attracted sightseers, and the canal wasn't strictly an industrial and transportation operation. In *Ambitious Appetites*, her book about dining and social life in early

Lockhouses were built of the same Seneca Creek Red Sandstone as the canal walls and whitewashed into trim homes where the lock keeper was always on call. John C. Riley and his family lived in Lockhouse 24, where he was the lockkeeper from 1892 until 1905, when his young daughter drowned in the canal. The family moved to a home across River Road, and Riley would rent rooms in the lockhouse to campers. *Courtesy Library of Congress.*

Washington, Barbara G. Carson recounted a country supper hosted by Colonel John Tayloe and his wife, Ann, who lived in one of D.C.'s most impressive homes, the Octagon House. The party drove out to the falls, "taking guns and fishing rods, 'everyone went their own way after their different amusement until three o'clock when…we dined on boards laid upon the rocks & seated upon the rocks.'" Enslaved women cooked a menu of "fish broiled on hot stones…cold meats, bread and cheese and oceans of wine, punch & brandy." They were entertained by a military band and enjoyed the "wild and romantic" landscape.

Later, canalboats shared the waterway with visitors who would come out for the scenery at Great Falls, to fish for carp and turtles (used to make turtle soup) or to canoe and camp. Lockkeeper Harvey Brant sold ice cream and sodas to weekenders and ran a canoe club along with tending the locks. The Swain family stayed on the canal after it turned from hauling into a national park, where they ran a seasonal refreshment stand.

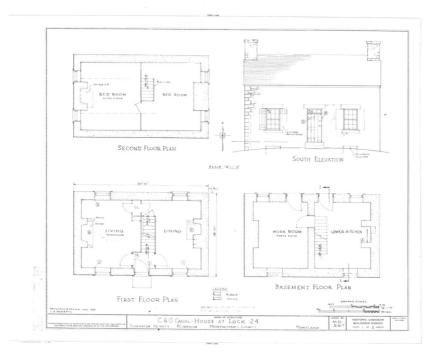

CANAL Packet Boat GEO. WASHINGTON.
The Packet Boat George Washington will com-
mence her daily trips to Crommelin and Seneca to-
morrow morning, leaving the temporary lock above
Georgetown at ½ past 7 o'clock, to return the same
evening. The proprietors will spare no effort on their
part to render satisfaction to all who patronize their
boat. They are provided with good teams, and every
arrangement is made in their boat and bar for the comfort of the public.

Parties wishing to make an excursion to either of the
above places, by giving short notice, will be accommodated in best style. Those who have not already
enjoyed the delight, which the scenery of the contiguous country, and the great work itself, (the Chesapeake
and Ohio Canal) afford, will now have the opportunity
of gratifying themselves.

    Fare to Crommelin   37½ cents.
    " to Seneca   50 cents.
        Same returning.

P. S. In a few days the proprietors hope to get their
Boat into Georgetown, when they will, until further
notice, leave the Market House, at the hour above
named, and return to the same spot.

        SAMUEL CUNNINGHAM,
          THOS. NOWLAN.
Georgetown, July 12—tf

Above: Life in a lockhouse was almost as snug as on a canalboat. This measured drawing of Lockhouse 24, completed for the Historic American Buildings Survey, shows shared spaces— living and dining—downstairs and two bedrooms upstairs, organized around a central stair. The earthen floor basement held another kitchen and a workroom. *Courtesy Library of Congress.*

Left: Canalboat day-trippers could enjoy "the scenery of the contiguous country, and the great work itself." *Courtesy Montgomery History.*

President Grover Cleveland made fishing excursions to Pennyfield's lock, where George and Martha Pennyfield ran a boardinghouse. Cleveland was an avid hunter and fisherman, and after he retired from the presidency, he wrote a book, *Fishing and Shooting Sketches*, in which he defended fishermen from charges of laziness and lying, decried the habit of shooting birds too small to eat and claimed it unsportsmanlike to shoot a sitting rabbit. Cleveland clearly valued time spent in nature: "Manifestly, if outdoor recreations are important to the individual and to the nation, and if there is danger of their neglect, every instrumentality should be heartily encouraged which aims to create and stimulate their indulgence in every form. Fortunately, the field is broad and furnishes a choice for all except those wilfully at fault. The sky and sun above the head, the soil beneath the feet, and outdoor air on every side are the indispensable requisites."

The earliest canal hospitality was offered in 1831 when the lockkeeper's house at Great Falls was expanded into a tavern. For a time, it was called Crommelin House, after the Dutchman who set up its financing. A steam-powered boat would carry day-trippers from Georgetown, although by 1853, the cranes, piping and cut stone for construction of the Washington Aqueduct had made the site less appealing for an afternoon in the country.

The county's country inns proved popular through the decades. Old Angler's Inn opened in 1860 and for a time served as a general store and post office. In *Days at Cabin John*, Edith Armstrong described driving out the Conduit Road (later McArthur Boulevard) in the 1920s and stopping at

SHAD. This fish is an anadromous herring—that is, like salmon, they spend their lives in salt water, returning to spawn in freshwater rivers, and they are high in fatty acids. They are bony, oily and delicious, and in early America shad was salted, pickled, planked and dismissed as inferior to pork. They were fished not for sport but for sale. In 1774, William Milnor of Philadelphia was advertising shad taken from a fishery in the "Patowmack" River, where they were promptly salted and barreled for travel. Native Americans caught shad in the Potomac using V-shaped weirs to corral the fish. Today, avid fishermen monitor the Potomac's temperature and water levels to judge the best time to cast a line.

The Hiking Club posed at the Great Falls Hotel, "a popular tourist attraction." *Courtesy Montgomery History.*

"the Anglers Club for a drink of its delicious water" drawn from a well surrounded by black walnut and persimmon trees. The club had been used for fifty years as a rendezvous for sportsmen. The ceiling was made of hand-hewn beams from the keels of abandoned canal barges.

In 1931, Normandie Farms was opened on land that was formerly the Myers Farm, developed as a country inn favored by Eleanor Roosevelt. In *The Annals of Sandy Spring*, W.H. Farquhar, in his report for 1871–72, recorded that "[a]n institution of this neighborhood…is the taking of summer boarders," who offered an easy income and came to rest under the trees and escape the summer heat. He warned, though, against the danger of adopting city customs such as frivolous fashions and amusements, heartless compliments and gaudy dress—"unsuited to rational country life." The tensions between farming and recreation and urban and rural were and are varied.

One of the biggest visitor attractions along the canal started out as one of the smallest. German immigrant Joseph Bobinger and his wife, Rosa, came to the area, drawn by work on the Washington Cabin John Bridge and aqueduct, where he signed on as a stonecutter. Rosa decided to set up a refreshment stand for workers where she sold cigars, snuff, cold drinks and pies. She eventually expanded into a boardinghouse, renovated from a construction shed.

This Historic American Buildings Survey record photograph of Great Falls Tavern, circa 1933, shows that the building shares the same rectangular massing as the lockhouses, but expressed here on a grander scale. Note the Coca-Cola sign in the lower left corner—the building was no longer a tavern, but it was still serving customers. *Courtesy Library of Congress.*

The canal was a popular outing, as the *Washington Post* wrote, "[O]ne could also go out the Conduit Road for breakfast or dinner at Cabin John, one of Washington's established amusements, which every visitor to the Nation's Capitol [*sic*] puts on his sightseeing programme." *Courtesy Library of Congress.*

Joseph had worked as a stonecutter and a head waiter, and in 1870, with a Riggs Bank loan, they bought one hundred acres on the west side of the bridge and built the Cabin John Bridge Hotel with twenty-five rooms. The real draw for day-trippers were Rosa's dinners, which cost one dollar and featured a specialty: Chicken à la Maryland: fried chicken in a brown gravy, topped with bacon and served with corn fritters. On the menu were typical Victorian-era dishes—oysters, potted grouse, sweetbreads—along with local specialties like buttermilk biscuits and smallmouth bass, which were held fresh in an enclosure in the creek until they were ready to be served with new potatoes and tartar sauce. The hotel served wines from John Reading's vineyards on both sides of Cabin John Creek and had a rathskeller that developed a risqué reputation.

After Joseph and Rosa died, their sons continued the hotel into its heyday from the 1890s to the 1900s. They added two banquet rooms and counted among their customers diplomats, cabinet members, congressmen and presidents, including Taft, Roosevelt and Wilson. Washingtonians were drawn to the hotel's lawns, gardens and gazebos. They could stroll a lover's lane path and enjoy musical entertainment.

From a snack shop, the hotel had grown into a massive operation. It included an icehouse, smokehouse, dairy, poultry coops, stables, gas house and one of the country's largest asparagus beds. The hotel baked its own bread and employed seventeen bartenders and forty waiters.

The hotel, its rathskeller and its small amusement park were leased to new owners in 1914, but Prohibition cut into the business, as did blue laws against Sunday operations. Those looking for recreation were drawn to the new country clubs and the Glen Echo amusement park on the east side of the bridge, connected to D.C. by a trolley line. The hotel's doors were locked in 1926, with all the fittings left in place, and over time the neglected hotel slowly deteriorated. A 1931 fire finished it off, taking plates, menus and records with it.

The hotel had drawn investors to the area who saw potential in the area's farmland. When Edwin Baltzley and his brother, Edward, purchased 516 acres overlooking the Potomac River, it was with a sharp eye for the growing movement of suburban development. Streetcar lines were making city connections quick and accessible, and there was more money to be made from house lots and hotels than from farming.

Edwin Baltzley worked as a government clerk, but he was also an inventor. His "culinary beater" was a labor-saving device that allowed cooks to easily beat eggs and whip cream. The brothers founded the

The 1870 menu highlighted one of the hotel's specialties, Maryland fried chicken—
fried chicken in a white cream sauce served with curled strips of bacon on top and corn
fritters. The dish was advertised as "fried spring chicken, Cabin John Style." *Courtesy
Montgomery History.*

Keystone Manufacturing Company in Philadelphia and earned a fortune
of $250,000, today equivalent to $12 million. They relocated to Washington
and established themselves as "dealers in real estate."

The Baltzleys envisioned a Chautauqua community with an educational
program of uplifting lectures and performances. They advertised Glen Echo
Park as a place with "No objectionable characters. No spiritous liquors."

The hotel's dinnerware, imported from Bavaria, Germany, was decorated with a dogwood blossom design on the edges, topped by the initials B.B., surrounding an image of the landmark Union Arch Bridge. The red, green and clear crystal goblets were Belgian imports. *Courtesy Montgomery History.*

From this illustrated view of the Cabin John Bridge Hotel, it's clear why the hotel was such an attraction—fluttering flags, romantic turrets, music, gardens, dining and drinking. *Courtesy Montgomery History.*

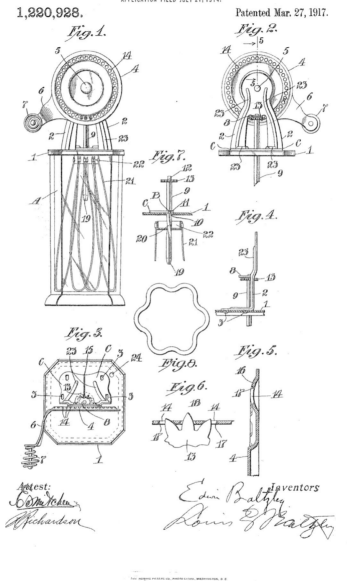

E. & L. E. BALTZLEY.
CULINARY BEATER.
APPLICATION FILED JULY 21, 1914.

1,220,928.

Patented Mar. 27, 1917.

Following the old saying, Edwin Baltzley "built a better mousetrap"—in his case, the Baltzley Culinary Beater, an invention that made him a fortune and allowed him to invest in real estate at Glen Echo. *Courtesy United States Patent Office.*

The Glen Echo summer streetcar (circa 1892) delivered visitors to the National Chautauqua and later to the Glen Echo Amusement Park. Edwin Baltzley's "baronial castle"—which indulged in a romantic architecture of turrets, chimneys and balconies—is visible in the background. *Courtesy Montgomery History.*

They encouraged sales by establishing the Glen Echo Railroad Company with a connection to Tenleytown and opening a café called PA-TOW-O-MECK. It opened in July 1890 with ceremonies and senators. The rustic-style log building was well furnished inside and drew customers who were then charmed into buying land.

Over time, the character of the park changed, with programming shifting from uplift to entertainment, with jugglers, prizefights and light opera. In 1899, the United Daughters of the Confederacy of Maryland and Virginia held an encampment at Glen Echo, warranting a speech from President William McKinley and a luncheon in the amphitheater of beef, bacon, hardtack and coffee.

In 1899, Glen Echo shifted fully to an amusement park, with mechanized rides, and the manager's boast of a new ride every year encouraged return visits. The park's picnic grounds attracted families as well as school groups and employee associations. Children enjoyed candy apples, cotton candy, popcorn, fruit punch and soft ice cream. As Offutt recorded, hot dogs were a dime, and meals served on the terrace cost between $0.60 and $1.25; a 1939 renovation added three restaurants and fast-food booths. If visitors preferred more adult entertainment—gambling, bootleg liquor and dancing—they could stop at one of the roadhouses along the canal and Conduit Road, including the Silver Spider, the Texas Tavern or the Rock-a-Way Inn.

The canal stopped operation after a 1924 flood and lay neglected by all but bootleggers until it was transferred from the B&O Railroad in 1938 to the federal government in exchange for a loan from the Reconstruction Finance Corporation. The National Park Service began a partial renovation, with the intent of making it a recreation area.

The area's reputation as a place for relaxation made it a place for weekend cottages and camps. In *Cabin John: Legends and Life of an Uncommon Place*, Judith Welles recalled childhood camping in one of the summer shacks. In 1912, there was no water or electricity, but they spent the days swimming, canoeing, fishing, collecting chestnuts and persimmons—they'd "bring a picnic lunch and stay all day." The 1925 census of the area reported eighty summer residents who could visit Tuohey's store for basics or ride the trolley to Georgetown. They could enjoy church socials, with cake sales and chicken dinners.

Residents and visitors were drawn by the area's rural character. The Tuoheys didn't sell milk because, even up until the Depression, most people kept a cow. In 1913, house lots in Cabin John Park advertised their advantages, including "fertile land, suitable truck patches, fine soil for apples; peaches, pears, plums; sweet Irish potatoes, chicken farms; grapes and melons."

It was the same at other spots along the canal. The cottages along the Seneca Creek were popular getaways but were swept away by a flood in the 1960s. Summer cottages on the Monocacy near the aqueduct bridge eventually attracted squatters, and in 1983, the area was cleared and renovated as part of the C&O Canal Park.

But before the canal could be established as a national park (the nation's longest and narrowest), there was interest in repurposing the canal as a parkway. Supreme Court justice William O. Douglas staved off its paving by taking an eight-day hike from Cumberland to D.C. The hike garnered attention and support for the canal as a natural environment and historic place. Its creation as a park proceeded in fits and starts, much the way it was originally built. Committees, plans, acts and piecemeal renovations culminated in its establishment as a national park in 1971.

Easily reachable by trolley line from the city, the Glen Echo Amusement Park offered the full experience—from a sedate carousel to a looping roller coaster—including fun food like popcorn. *Courtesy Library of Congress.*

The canal remains a unique place in Montgomery County, and while it no longer bustles with industry and commerce, during an early morning summer walk, when birdsong drowns out the Beltway, you can imagine the gardens and kitchens of the neighborhoods along the canal and how they might be called on to create the kind of community supper described by Edith Martin Armstrong in her 1958 book, *Days at Cabin John*:

> *Long boards on trestles formed tables covered with snow-white damask and centered with tight bouquets of stubby zinnias and marigolds stuffed into tall glasses. On each were homemade jellies and pickles of various kinds,*

glass bowls of applesauce, generous quantities of potato salad and slaw, and platters heaped with tempting slices of ham. Around and about the room, women with plain and fancy aprons carried plates of fried chicken and sugar corn. Some were chatting over steaming kettles, and others were cutting large, luscious-looking pies.

"Mrs. Hebbs, your chicken is wonderful." I was making my way around a drumstick. "I'd like to have you give me a few lessons in frying."

She flushed a little. "There's nothin' special to it. You just fry."

A Cupboard in the Corner—Boatman's Bean Soup with Rivvels
Serves 6 to 8

Rivvels are a Pennsylvania Dutch dish—an on-the-fly kind of spaetzle, a quick noodle, a simple dumpling. The dough is cut directly into the soup, where it cooks in the broth, adding body and flavor. As Theodore Lizer recalled in his oral history for Home on the Canal, *"We ate a lot of bean soup," and they made their soup with rivvels. "Take some flour in a dish, break an egg in it, stir it all up, let it get heavy, keep working it till it gets heavy. Just flour and egg; just like you were going to make pot pie dough. That's all you use—egg; no water. Then it'll all get up in a bump, and you pinch off little pieces about as big as the end of your finger and keep dropping them in the bean soup. It's yellow; the eggs made the flour yellow. And that's what they called rivvels."*

For the soup:
I pound dried great northern beans or navy beans
2 quarts water
I medium waxy potato, diced
I large onion, chopped
I large hambone or ham hocks; cut the lean meat off and add it to the soup pot
I pint canned tomatoes or 4 large ripe tomatoes, cut up

For the rivvels:
½ to ¾ cup white flour
Pinch of salt

Pinch of pepper
1 egg

To make the soup, soak the beans overnight and drain. In a large pot, put the beans, water, potatoes, onion and hambone. Cook until the potatoes are done but still firm. Add the tomatoes and cook for 30 minutes more. Add more water as needed as the beans cook.

While the soup simmers, make the rivvel dough. Blend ½ cup of flour with the salt and pepper and then stir in the egg, adding flour a spoonful at a time, to form a sticky but pinchable dough. Pinch off nickel-sized pieces and drop them into simmering soup. Cook until the rivvels are shiny and a bit chewy, about 2 to 4 minutes.

Note: Potatoes and rivvels make for a hearty soup. If you're not guiding a canalboat through the locks, you can choose to include one or the other in your soup.

Chapter 4

A QUAKER KITCHEN

Montgomery County has a particular self-regard, a not unjustified pride in its history and achievements. It's a stance that may have been established by the well-chronicled Quaker communities of Sandy Spring and Brookeville. *The Annals of Sandy Spring* is a twenty-year recounting of farms and families—yields of both crops and children. Roger Brook Farquhar, a descendant of this community, wrote in *Old Homes and History* of plucky original settlers, prospering into estates.

Much of their work and effort can be told through their farms and tables. These chroniclers take a justified pride in returning fertility to tobacco-spent soils, using "scientific farming" techniques, technological advances and social improvements.

Like their Tidewater and lower Potomac neighbors, Montgomery County's original farmers grew tobacco as well as food crops like their upper Potomac and Frederick neighbors. Initially, tobacco was a prosperous pursuit, with demand from European markets, and nearby ports in Georgetown and Alexandria were set up to warehouse, price and ship the leaves. With high market prices, estate owners willing to use enslaved labor could turn their lands to cash crops and spend the spoils on hunting and socializing.

Tobacco is a labor-intensive crop. As Lord Baltimore was informed in 1729, it "leaves no room for anything else; it requires the attendance of all our hands and exacts all their labor, the whole year-round." It could be cost-effective when slaves did the work of planting, growing, drying and baling and if the market demand would support a good sales price. Six years after its founding, the county's population was 10,011 White and 4,407 Black. Tobacco planting in Montgomery was less intensive than in the Tidewater, leading to smaller estates and fewer slaves, but nonetheless, it established a planter class that would hold political power into the early twentieth century.

Tobacco growing also directed a pattern of development—large plantations rather than smaller farmsteads centered on towns. As Gutheim wrote, "The tobacco civilization stamped the landscape, originated social habits…good manners and sharp trading, hard riding and soft living."

Tobacco is also hard on the soil, pulling out nitrogen, a nutrient that plants need to thrive. With no way to replace or retain the nitrogen through fertilizers or farming practices, the soil lost its ability to produce crops. When the market crashed—tobacco was glutting the market and prices dropped—Montgomery County farms were poorly positioned to switch to other crops.

Farms reached their lowest point around the 1830s; poor soils couldn't sustain a family. T.H.S. Boyd wrote, "The land would no longer yield an increase, and they made no attempt at renovating and improving the soil, and

An aerial view of the Walden King Farm in 1946, where "[t]obacco was the main crop, some grain also." In recounting her life in Clarksburg, Gloria King Winter recalled that her father's cousin, John Glaze, was the last Montgomery County farmer to raise tobacco. Her parents "mostly raised crops, flowering plants and produce." Even when her parents sold off some of their property to a developer, they kept ten acres where her mother raised produce to sell at the Farm Women's Market. *Courtesy Montgomery History.*

Montgomery lands became a synonym for poverty." There are descriptions of fallen fence rows, neglected farmhouses and weedy fields. Sons chose to move west to literally greener pastures in Ohio and Kentucky.

An 1849 article in the African American newspaper the *National Era* confirms that despite a nearby market in the District of Columbia connected by decent roads, "farming in Maryland and Virginia, as heretofore conducted, has not on the whole been profitable, may be inferred from the fact that vast numbers of people in both States are willing to sell their lands, at such prices as they can get, and seek their fortunes elsewhere."

This author speculates that it was not the inherent quality of land prompting this migration: "It is not in the land; for where that is left with nature's planting, it produces noble trees; and where it is well cultivated by man, it rewards the labor by abundant harvests of corn and wheat." "Well cultivated" is the key phrase here and one that resonates for today's farmers who are attentive to their soil and farms' operations. The author posits that land cultivated by "unwilling hands"—that is, enslaved labor—is sloppily ploughed and seeded, yielding "continually lessening harvests, till exhaustion follows, and the field is deserted for another, to be in like manner subjected to the depleting process." Then as now, sustainability encompasses not only the soil but also people and the community and economy they create.

The *National Era* was making a political point—that enslaved labor was a false economy, one that had costs for the land and the community. But the author had confidence that under "proper tillage" the land has a capacity for "a high degree of agricultural improvement." It was a confidence shared by the local Quaker community, whose members shared information and advanced technology to return fertility to county farms.

In *History of Western Maryland*, Scharf noted that "[m]uch of the successful farming of this county has been due to the free use of lime. The soils being generally sour require the addition of this substance or plaster of Paris.... Some of the farmers...near the line of the Chesapeake and Ohio Canal, transport the limestone to their farms where they burn it in kilns and then offer the surplus for sale to their neighbors."

The Quaker community ranged over Pennsylvania, Delaware and Maryland. In Montgomery County, they were a practical and progressive group. The Sandy Spring Quakers were instrumental in agricultural reform, including crop rotation, diversified crops and mechanization. Another technique, fertilizing the soil with powdered limestone, became known as the Loudoun method, where it took hold first and was brought to Montgomery by Thomas Moore, who married into the Brooke family.

Moore helped Sandy Spring become a center for agricultural knowledge, starting by reclaiming his own farm and generating high yields using a variety of techniques, including deep ploughing undertaken in the early spring, eight to eleven inches deep, to break up the soil. Moore also rotated crops, applied manure and plaster to return nutrients and planted buckwheat and clover cover crops, allowing a fallow year for the soil to replenish. By 1843, some farmers could afford to buy nitrogen-rich guano imported into Baltimore supported with lime, marl (a carbonate-rich mudstone), bonemeal and manure. But milling and shipping made fertilizers expensive, and many farmers relied instead on "scientific" farming practices like deep plowing and crop rotation until the 1870s, when the B&O's Metropolitan Branch could deliver less expensive lime in large quantities.

In *History of Western Maryland*, Scharf described the success of these efforts on Thomas Moore's farm: "Persons came from long distances to see his farm and to witness the deep plowing with the mammoth plow of his own invention, his fine stock of cattle in the fields of red clover, his meadows of timothy, fine fields of corn, the ground yellow with pumpkins, and the large pen of small-bone hogs fattened on pumpkins, corn and slop boiled in a box."

With his brother-in-law, Isaac Briggs, a teacher and engineer, Moore started the Sandy Spring Farmers' Society "to enlarge our sphere of knowledge by a free communication of individual experiences and opinion either by written essays or otherwise; to cultivate a spirit of scientific enquiry and solid improvements particularly in the Theory and Practice of Agriculture and to strengthen the benevolent ties which bind us together." In 1802, the society named James Madison as an honorary corresponding member to whom it proposed expanding the group into the American Board of Agriculture, which first met in 1803, with Madison elected president. The American Board of Agriculture was a forerunner of the federal Department of Agriculture.

In the 1840s, in response to the decline in farming success, farmers societies were established around the county to share information and advice—in Brookeville and Sandy Spring, as well as in the Medley District on the county's western edge.

It was also a congenial community that socialized at the table. In *Memories of Eighty Years*, Mary Coffin Brooke recalled farm life and family suppers. Of a winter visit to cousins the night before her wedding to William S. Brooke, she noted, "We were chilled from our long ride, and I will never forget how I enjoyed the bright open fire and the nice hot supper. Cousin

While livestock and horse racing were the main features of the fair, the 1876 program lists the categories for the Culinary Department, where cooks could show their skills in homemade light bread, biscuits, rolls, rusk, sponge cake, pound cake, jelly cakes, jellies, canned fruits, preserves, pickles, catsup, vinegar, hard soap, soft soap, grape wine, blackberry wine and currant wine, among others. *Courtesy Montgomery History.*

Ellen Farquhar, who was there also, had remembered that I liked stewed chicken and flannel cakes, and we had both."

Coffin Brooke took a hand in running their farm, recording what they produced for market: "When I went to Avon, Willie had several cows, but I begged him to increase the number and build a modern dairy, which he did, and for several years we made about sixty pounds of butter each week, which was sold in Washington for from forty-five to fifty cents per pound." And like most county farms, they grew fruit and vegetables for their own use and to sell: "Willie was very fond of gardening, and we always had an abundance of vegetables, and the apples and peach orchards gave us more fruit that we could use."

Mary Coffin Brooke thought her life and community were worth recording and described the atmosphere of this Quaker community as "progressive and educational." Sandy Spring was a center of self-improvement efforts, including the establishment of a subscription library and fire insurance society. In the 1930s, its Farmers' Convention would be the source of the county government's change to a county manager system and home rule charter.

THE MONTGOMERY COUNTY AGRICULTURAL FAIR

The phrase "county fair" brings to mind Ferris wheels, crowds and a lot of fried food, and early fairs certainly had a social and recreational component, but they also offered some friendly competition and proof of agricultural techniques.

As Scharf pointed out in *History of Western Maryland*, "No county in the State had given more careful and intelligent study to the development of the science of agriculture. The people of Montgomery are among the most cultured in Maryland, and for many years have seen and profited by the advantages of co-operation and interchanges of views upon their paramount industry, the cultivation of the soil."

The county's first agricultural fair was held on September 12 and 13, 1822, in Rockville and put a particular emphasis on judging sheep, swine and cattle. The fair became a more organized event when held by the Montgomery County Agricultural Society, beginning in 1846 on the site of what is now Richard Montgomery High School. Roger Brooke Farquhar described creating the new fairgrounds on sixty-four acres northwest of Gaithersburg as a "cooperative project," with a committee organizing supplies and labor. It took two thousand men to build the forty-four buildings that would house "a worthy successor to the Rockville Fair."

Just before the Civil War, Anna Brooke Farquhar wrote an essay on her school class's visit to the fair in 1855. She described a nearly nine-mile carriage ride that took two hours on a hot day that called for a refreshing drink of cold water when they arrived. During their stop in the first tent, they looked at "the many articles for exhibition," including those classified as "household manufacture"—quilts, knit spreads, linsey "and a great variety of fancy articles," as well as butter, bread "and other eatables." They examined the cattle, but Anna was most taken with the horses: "Some of them were so beautiful, that it was right hard to leave them."

So, the morning passed, and the group went to the shaded woods "where a very nice dinner was prepared for us." But they seemed most interested in cold water and "could scarcely get enough of the article to satisfy our thirst." After lunch, some enjoyed a speech on botany, and the premiums were awarded "to those who had the good luck to get any."

During the Civil War, the fairgrounds became Camp Lincoln, eventually the site of twenty thousand Union troops and everything it took to support them. They were tasked with protecting the C&O Canal and the county's border with Virginia. As Montgomery was home to Southern sympathizers, the troops were an occupying army that questioned residents about their sympathies and, because food was scarce, requisitioned what they needed.

After the Civil War, the fair began again, drawing farmers from across the region. In 1870, the Sandy Spring Horticultural Society abandoned its own event to concentrate on "the County Fair soon to take place in Rockville." W.H. Farquhar judged this county-wide agricultural fair to be a good thing but the accompanying horse races a bad thing. He encouraged fewer parties that season to check the growing evil of late hours. Nonetheless, in 1872, the Metropolitan Branch delivered hundreds of visitors, drawn to the fair as a social occasion.

Entries for the 1876 fair could be made in a wide variety of categories, including Horses, Cattle, Sheep, Hogs, Poultry, Dairy, Wheat Crops, Corn Crops, Seed, Flour, Tobacco, Machinery and Agricultural Implements, Carriages (Saddle and Harness), Vegetables, Flowers, Home-made Fabrics, Hams and the Culinary Department. Over the years, the society's ledgers document premiums paid for potatoes, cucumbers, lima beans, pumpkins, carrots, beets, onions and turnips.

In 1932, the fair organization was in financial trouble and held a public sale of the buildings and grounds. In 1949, the fair was resurrected at the Gaithersburg fairgrounds, with another cooperative effort to construct twelve buildings. That year, the fair featured 343 exhibitors and 1,308 exhibits and paid $5,083 in premiums.

In 1961, there were 1,819 exhibitors, 8,707 exhibits and $30,034 in premiums and included 4-H for the first time. Today, the fair is operated by the Montgomery County Agricultural Center, with the help of thousands of volunteers, sponsors and participants. If you're feeling confident in your home arts, enter in one of three departments, twenty-eight divisions and numerous classes that include preserved vegetables, sauces, fresh and aged cheeses, corn relish, dried meat, iced and un-iced cakes, bar cookies and fruit pies.

Michael Twitty, in his article on "Foodways in Montgomery County" for the *Montgomery County Story*, described the period between 1800 and 1870 as one where county farms transitioned from tobacco to grains, as well as orchards, dairies and truck gardens. Twitty also described the "rural machine" of individual farms that were family businesses, with jobs and responsibilities for men, women and children. The considerations of an operational farm, a place not just for a view but for a livelihood, can be seen in this 1849 advertisement in the *National Era*:

> *Norwood is beautifully situated on the turnpike leading from Georgetown to Rockville, four miles from the former place, and contains one hundred and sixty-four acres of land, all of which is enclosed and laid off into fields, and about eight acres is set in timothy, clover, and wheat. There are on the premises a new, commodious, and handsome dwelling, suitable for a gentleman of large family, and a pump of pure water in the kitchen yard. The grounds around the building are tastefully laid off, barn with stabling for a number of horses and cattle, corn-house, ice-house, dairy, &c.; also, an extensive orchard of fruit trees, of select quality, in full bearing—apple, pear, peach, plum, cherry, quince, grape, &c. The land is well adapted to the cultivation of corn, wheat, oats, and grass, and, from its proximity to Washington and Georgetown, it might be made a valuable dairy farm. The situation is remarkably healthy, and might be used advantageously as a place of resort for families from Washington and Georgetown during the sickly season. The tract can be divided into fifty-acre farms, to suit purchasers, if desired. Should the property not be disposed of previously, it will be offered at public sale, on the premises, on Thursday, May 10, 1849, at four o'clock, P.M.*

More than land with a house, each aspect of its operation is spelled out—water source, stabling, icehouse, dairy, orchard, fields—with the potential as a resort or subdivision. Farming was not a single thing—one crop, one way of operating—but a balanced economy to support a family.

This view of the farm as an economic enterprise applies to family farms and to larger estates. Of a different class, Nelly Custis Lewis, granddaughter and adopted daughter of Martha Custis and George Washington, was raised at Mount Vernon, where she learned to manage enslaved servants, treat guests, ensure food supply, serve appropriate food, converse, dress, behave and develop "accomplishments."

In her housekeeping book, she recorded cookery, medicinal recipes and craft instructions, as well as notes of debts and a laundry list. A recipe for sponge cake, recorded as coming from "Mrs. P," is possibly contributed by her sister, Martha Parke Custis Peter, mistress of Montevideo.

In 1969, editor of the *Montgomery County Story* Martha Sprigg Poole described a similar farm layout: main house, tenant house, barn/silo/corn crib, chicken coop and yard and hog lot, as well as the work required to feed a farm family. "Cooking was preceded by preparing food. Chickens, for instance, had to be killed, plucked and cleaned. Vegetables must be gathered from the garden. The stove was heated by chunks of wood which had to be fed to the stove continually. No frozen or packaged food! No electric appliances."

And no supermarkets, so the family garden had to provide food year-round, either eaten fresh when ripe and pickled or preserved to last through the winter. The fat that separated to the top of the milk would be skimmed and churned into butter, which would be portioned, wrapped and kept cool in a springhouse. "Butter was often traded at the County Store for staples such as sugar, salt, coffee, etc."

She went on to recount family responsibilities. "The chicken department on a farm was usually in feminine hands. The poultry had to be fed— sometimes with the shelled corn which the kids had taken from the ears. Eggs were gathered daily for family use. They too were often traded at the store."

T.H.S. Boyd devoted a chapter to peach production, and Diane Williams, who grew up in Sandy Spring on her family's farmland, recalled peach, pear and apple trees. Sprigg Poole wrote, "Probably there was an orchard with an assortment of apple, pear, peach, plum, and cherry trees for family use. Here too, the products were used as they became ripe and stored where possible; some fruit would be canned and pickled and some apples would be made into cider which might be drunk as such or made into vinegar."

In *A Grateful Remembrance*, the authors described a typical county farm as a mix of crops, some grown to sell and some grown to support the family: "Nearly every farm in the County had a flock of six to 20 sheep, three or four dairy cows, a horse or two, and 12 hogs. Draft oxen were no longer common. Many farms were organized to meet family needs, with a small surplus for market. Farmers hauled grain to one of the neighborhood grist mills to get flour and cornmeal custom ground. They shipped another 50 or 100 bushels to Washington or Baltimore for sale."

PEACHES. Originally from China, peaches were spread to the Mediterranean by the Romans and to New World by the Spanish, where they were naturalized and cultivated by Native Americans. After the Civil War, U.S. peaches were hybridized into large, round fruits with blushed skin and yellow flesh. T.H.S. Boyd noted that peach cultivation moved to Montgomery County from the exhausted soils on the Eastern Shore and recorded the evocatively named varieties grown in Montgomery County and their seasons: Beatrice, mid-July; Hale's Early, about July 25; Hollis' Early, August 1; Walter's Early or Mountain Rose, August 5; Early York, August 7; Crawford's Early, August 10; Mary's Choice, August 15; Druid Hill, Harkins' Seedling, Old Mixon Free and Stump the World, August 17–18; Crawford's Late, August 20; Jaques, Monmouth Melacaton and Susquehanna, August 20; Magnum Bonum, late August; Late Heath Cling-stone, September 12; and Bear's Smock, the latest peach. In *The Annals of Sandy Spring*, Farquhar wrote in 1878 that on March 10, "A little peach tree in the front yard, with south exposure, has full bloom on it. Apricot is in bloom." On March 29, the thermometer fell to twenty-nine degrees, and peach blossoms were killed in many places. On the thirty-first, "the wind blew lionlike."

While each farm was its own small industry, beyond the soil, they relied on innovations in technology and farm practices to be successful, inventions like threshers and binders. Scientific approaches in hybridized plants and carefully bred livestock included Mediterranean and Purplestraw wheat hybrids in 1822 and Zimmerman wheat in 1837. Farmers tested improved nursery stock, fruit tree varieties and livestock breeds for their resiliency in the area's climate and the particular characteristics of a given farm.

Henry Blair farmed in the Silver Spring area, and he was the second Black man to receive a U.S. patent, in 1834 for a corn planter. His second patent was for a cotton planter. Blades would cut a furrow, and a cylinder behind would drop in seed. Like many farmers, he was looking for efficiency and lightened load. Patents reveal the day-to-day work of life, and the files include patents for a wagon brake, a prototype sulky (a single-person,

A distinctive piece of Montgomery County's landscape—Sugarloaf Mountain—is named for a food. Refined sugar was part of the colonial-era Triangle Trade between Europe and the New World. Enslaved people from Africa were sold to sugar plantation owners in the Caribbean, who sold raw sugar to Europe, which sold refined sugar back to its trading partners. *Courtesy George Kousoulas.*

Native diets were varied with local ingredients and seasonal foods. Trout and sumac were available in nearly every part of the country and create a dish that can be cooked and appreciated today. *Courtesy George Kousoulas.*

Plants foraged from forests and fields—wild carrot, milkweed, chickweed, sassafras—added flavor and nutrition to Native American dishes. *Courtesy George Kousoulas.*

Lockhouse keepers and their families were part of the canal's economy. Lockkeeper Harvey Brant caught and sold eels. He bought grain off the boats to fatten his hogs and ran a canoe rental business. *Courtesy George Kousoulas.*

Meals on the canalboats were limited to what you could carry and what you might pick up along the way. A slow simmered soup of dried beans and cured meat was easy to cook and filling. Once in Georgetown, the boatmen might treat themselves to a steak, and the children would take a dime or quarter and buy candy or a banana split. *Courtesy George Kousoulas.*

Great Falls of Potomac (N°1) near Washington, D.C.

From Washington, D.C.'s earliest settlement, Great Falls was a landmark where navigation stopped. But as this 1908 postcard shows, it was also a scenic attraction. "The Great Falls of the Potomac are fourteen miles above Washington. The Falls are formed by the waters forcing a passage through a stupendous ridge of granite. The descent is eighty feet in a distance of two miles. The point is a favorite excursion spot and is reached by trolley from Washington." *Courtesy Montgomery History.*

9647   CABIN JOHN BRIDGE, WASHINGTON, D. C.

This image is one of seven postcards, issued at the turn of the nineteenth century, in Montgomery History's collection. They have slightly different formats, but all the images reflect the fact that the Cabin John Bridge was an attraction—the "great bridge is seven miles from Georgetown and is recognized as the largest stone arch in existence." *Courtesy Montgomery History.*

In the "Introductory Address" of *Domestic Cookery*, Elizabeth Ellicott Lea explained her position: "entering, early in life upon the train of duties, was frequently embarrassed by her ignorance of domestic affairs." Accordingly, she supplied not "elegant preparations" but "the far more useful part of household duties." *Courtesy George Kousoulas.*

Brookeville, founded in 1794, was laid out with fifty-six lots on two main streets, Market and High, and four side streets. T.H.S. Boyd described it in his history as a "fashionable resort" "pleasantly located in one of the richest sections of the County." Summer visitors were drawn by "the restorative qualities of a strong Chalybeate Spring," and the town's services included a postmaster, blacksmiths, carpenter, carriages and wagons, merchants, harness, millers, watchmaker, farmers, physicians, shoemakers and a seamstress. *Courtesy George Kousoulas.*

When Mrs. Frances Trollope visited America in 1830, she made sharp observations about daily life, including a description of refreshments offered during a visit to a Montgomery County farm. The hostess's "female slave set out the great table, and placed upon it cups of the very coarsest blue ware, a little brown sugar in one, and a tiny drop of milk in another; no butter, though the lady assured us she has a 'deary' and two cows. Instead of butter, she 'hoped we would fix a little relish with our crackers,' in ancient English, eat salt meat and dry biscuits. Such was the fare, and for guests that certainly were intended to be honoured." *Courtesy George Kousoulas.*

This is one of Mrs. Spencer Watkins's recipes from the *Up-to-Date Cookbook of Tested Recipes* and is a departure from the sturdy farm cooking of Elizabeth Ellicott Lea. These are dishes that convey status and wealth. *Courtesy George Kousoulas.*

The Riley plantation, where Josiah Henson was enslaved, was eventually subdivided into suburban house lots, leaving the original house in place. County Parks archaeological digs have revealed clues to life on the farm. In 2021, reenactors at the Josiah Henson Museum and Park Public Day tell the stories only now being recovered. *Courtesy George Kousoulas.*

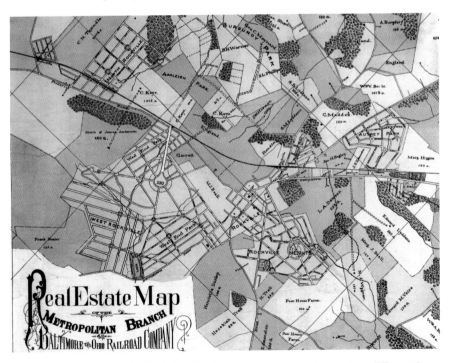

As the 1890 map shows, the Rockville Fair Grounds were convenient to the rail line and the site of other community celebrations, notably an 1876 centennial celebration of the county's founding, which featured speeches and, as T.H.S. Boyd recorded, a display of "relics and curiosities, giving a faithful reflex of the past." *Courtesy Library of Congress.*

"Food is Ammunition—Don't Waste It." The production of food and the waging of war are intimately connected. Siege tactics, destroying transportation connections and the battles fought on farm fields have, through history, been weapons of war. *Courtesy Library of Congress.*

"Uncle Sam Says Garden to Cut Food Costs." War-fighting and food production are distant from many of our lives, but during World War I and World War II, Montgomery County residents were drafted into the war effort in their own kitchens, encouraged to grow vegetables, eat less sugar and flour and not waste food. *Courtesy Library of Congress.*

During World War I, members of the Women's Land Army were issued a uniform of brimmed hats, blue overalls, a work shirt and gloves—designed to be practical and provide a sense of social cohesion. *Courtesy Montgomery History.*

Despite her sharp observations of Montgomery County farms, Mrs. Trollope found a luxury of summer fruit—"Strawberries of the richest flavour," a profusion of cherries for "all who would take the trouble to gather it" and every hedgerow planted with peaches. Fred van Hoesen, the county extension agent, took this picture of carefully sorted apples. *Courtesy Montgomery History.*

Many county businesses used their rural surroundings to sell their unique value. "At the Olney Inn traditions of cooking Maryland's finest farm foods prevail. The freshest and choicest of everything is selected—then painstaking care preserves the delicate natural flavors. Open daily, noon to nine o'clock, April–December, for Luncheon, Tea and Dinner. Visit Olney Inn, Miami Beach, Florida December–April." *Courtesy Montgomery History.*

Beautiful Countryside, Surrounded by Outstanding Dairy Farms
Only Twenty Minutes to Washington

From its earliest days, Montgomery County offered a country respite, attracting visitors for riverside picnics, a packet boat day trip, a drive out the Conduit Road for supper and a trolley ride to an amusement park. Early in the automobile era, Gaithersburg could offer a day in the country. *Courtesy Montgomery History.*

City and country complement each other. "Twilight Dinner in a Corner of the Garden of Mrs. K's Toll House Tavern, in Suburban Washington, 8 miles from the White House, on U.S. Route 29. This 'Old Maryland Tavern' is Open Daily All Year for Teas, Luncheons, generous Country Dinners and Sunday Breakfast." *Courtesy Montgomery History.*

Above: J. Willard Marriott started his business selling cold root beer during Washington's hot summers and soon diversified his menu with tamales and chili recipes his wife, Alice, got from the Mexican embassy. The Hot Shoppes was the first drive-in restaurant, and both dishes and service were based on corporate standards. *Courtesy George Kousoulas.*

Left: There were once more than five hundred dairy farms in Montgomery County delivering to creameries and markets. Sycamore Farms Dairy in Rockville was operated by Daisy and Harry Beard in the early twentieth century until their heirs sold the property to a developer, who subdivided it into house lots in 1948. Now the industry's local history and artifacts are collected at the Mooseum. *Courtesy Richard Rowe.*

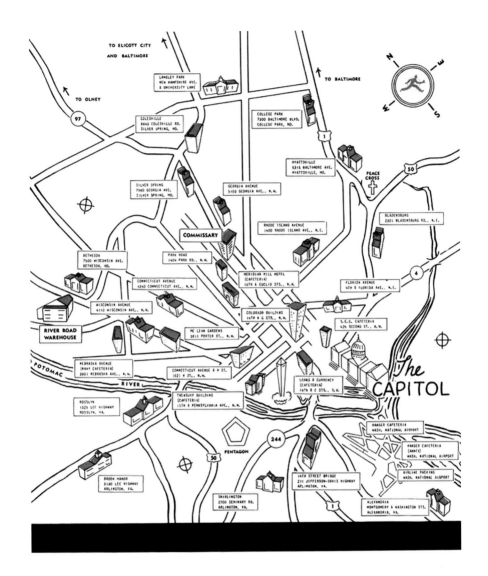

HOT SHOPPES "ALL AROUND THE TOWN!"

This 1954 map of Hot Shoppes locations in the D.C. region illustrates how Marriott located restaurants to catch customers—along busy roadways and where customers congregated in government buildings like the Securities and Exchange Commission cafeteria. *Courtesy Marriott Corporate Archives.*

As it has always been, the county's annual Agricultural Fair is a community event, a time for politicking, doing business and socializing. *Courtesy Digital Maryland, Governor Press Office.*

The future of farming in Montgomery County will certainly include making room for farms in unexpected places—a suburban house lot, a public park or the roof of a downtown building. *Courtesy George Kousoulas.*

Agriculture has an economic role as well as entertainment and educational roles. Few children participate in their family's food production, but at Calleva, campers can learn about growing and cooking food. *Courtesy Christopher Knowles Photography.*

Historian Frederick Gutheim lived in Dickerson at Mount Ephraim, which he purchased in 1941, enjoying a view of Sugarloaf Mountain. The house has a long history, built by Harris Ephraim circa 1866, who was the community's storekeeper. This crossroads included a post office, tavern and blacksmith's shop. *Courtesy Montgomery History.*

During the Depression, the federal government employed artists across the country to depict local landmarks in civic buildings. This view of Sugarloaf Mountain is in the Rockville Post Office. *Courtesy Barbara Grunbaum.*

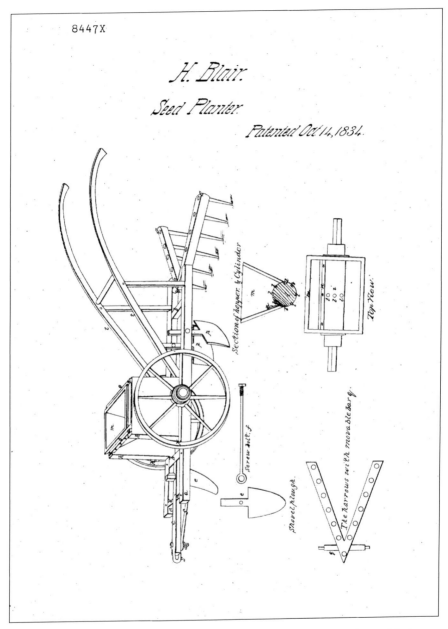

The four-page patent description of Henry Blair's corn planter describes the machine's form, with each part's function and measurement, and its operation. *Courtesy United States Patent Office.*

lightweight carriage), a weatherproof mail carriage, a bellows-powered churn, potato diggers, harvesting and corn cutting apparatuses and cement for lining oil barrels.

The patent records listed Blair as a "colored man," and whether he was free or enslaved, the federal government allowed him to hold a patent. In 1857, a slave owner challenged the law, claiming that he owned "all the fruits of the slave's labor," including inventions. In 1858, the law was changed, stating that because slaves weren't citizens, they couldn't hold patents. The law wasn't changed again until 1871, to grant all men (and women) patent rights.

A patent was also granted to Thomas Moore of Brookeville in 1803 for a type of refrigerator meant to deliver butter to market in Georgetown. His invention was an oval cedar box about eighteen inches deep. A squared tin box was placed inside that could hold twenty-two one-pound blocks of butter. Ice was packed around the box, and the whole was wrapped in rabbit pelts and covered with coarse woolen cloth. Despite the twenty-mile ride on horseback, the butter arrived firm and with enough ice to give each customer a small piece for the final trip to the table. This result allowed Moore to charge a higher price.

Moore invited Thomas Jefferson, who was interested in food and innovation, to see the refrigerator, and Jefferson sketched it on the corner of the invitation. Two years later, his memorandum book notes, "Paid Isaac Briggs for Thos. Moore 13.D. for a refrigerator."

Jefferson may have been an early adopter, but not everyone in his family thought the invention was worth the trouble. In a letter describing a trip to Poplar Forest in 1819, his granddaughter Ellen wrote, "Grand papa insisted on our using that filthy cooler, (refrigerator, I believe he calls it), which wasted our small stock of ice, and gave us butter that run about the plate so that we could scarcely catch it."

According to Scharf, Moore eventually made larger "refrigeratories" for dairies and families. His modification used two square cedar boxes, one within the other, with the space between packed with pulverized charcoal. A tin box attached to the inner lid of the smaller box contained the ice, and the whole was covered with a woolen cloth. Moore's refrigerator, noted Scharf, was used by "some heads of departments, and other citizens of the District of Columbia who had ice-houses." After fourteen years, Moore's patent expired, and he didn't renew it. Since not many people had regular access to ice, his invention had gone out of use.

[1802, June 21]

Thomas Moore respectfully invites the President of the United States to examine the condition of Butter in a new-invented Refrigeratory. put in the 21 Inst at 6 Oclock P.M. 20 miles distant from Washington

Retreat 6 mo 21st 1802

the wal was cooper's work
the inner parrallelogram was a box of tin
turned down on the top and trimmed to
the oval. a. and b. were 2 square holes
at which ice was put into the vacuity
between the tin & wood, the butter being
in the tin. 21376

Above: Thomas Moore's invitation to Thomas Jefferson to view the "refrigeratory" includes Jefferson's sketch of the invention. Moore received a patent for it in January 1803, but those records were lost in an 1836 fire, so no original drawing exists. *Courtesy Library of Congress, Manuscripts Division.*

Left: Elizabeth Ellicott Lea began assembling a household guide for herself, with recipes from relatives and family cookbooks, as well as contemporary published sources, in 1821 as a young married woman in Delaware. In 1823, she moved to Walnut Hill, a two-hundred-acre Montgomery County farm she had inherited that was near the Quaker communities of Brookeville and Sandy Spring in Montgomery County, Maryland. Her household guide would be published as *Domestic Cookery* in 1845. *Courtesy Sandy Spring Museum Archives.*

Another member of this practical and progressive community was Elizabeth Ellicott Lea, author of the 1845 *Domestic Cookery, Useful Receipts and Hints to Young Housekeepers*, which today remains a portrait of mid-Atlantic cooking in the early nineteenth century.

Lea began her manuscript in 1821 while a young married woman in Delaware, as a guide for herself, with recipes from relatives and family cookbooks, as well as contemporary published sources. In 1823, she moved to Walnut Hill, a two-hundred-acre Montgomery County farm she had inherited that was near the Quaker communities of Brookeville and Sandy Spring.

By 1842, her personal cookbook had grown in the number of recipes, and two manuscripts were created—one for her and one for her married daughter. In 1845, it was commercially printed by a Baltimore doctor, and in 1847 a publisher took it on. A second edition enlarged the book from 180 to 247 pages. A third edition in 1851 totaled 310 pages and included non-culinary information such as how to work with servants. By 1879, it was out of print, after nineteen editions.

Historian and author William Woys Weaver has combed through Lea's book and her notes. In his introduction to *A Quaker Woman's Cookbook: The Domestic Cookery of Elizabeth Ellicott Lea*, he supposes that Lea had a personal reason for continuing the cookbook. Her own early widowhood left her with responsibilities that she was unprepared for, and she didn't want her newly married daughter to face the same situation. She hoped that with attention to the recipes and housekeeping advice in her "humble little volume…many of the cares attendant on a country or city life, may be materially lessened."

These household skills were vital to the family's and farm's success. If a batch of dried corn or green beans preserved in a brine spoils, there's no easy way to make it up. The family will do without that season and will have to shoulder the expense of ruined crops and wasted work. The partnership between field and hearth reflect Twitty's description of the farmstead as a small industry and home skills—dairy sent to market, butter mints sold by the Montgomery County Farmwomen during the Depression or today's farm-based, value-added products—all creating a valuable infusion of cash into the family's account.

Nelly Custis Lewis ran her farm with enslaved labor and was of a different class than Lea, but they had some household chores in common. Both women needed to feed a crew of family and workers every day. They kept meat smokehouses, milled flour stores and a springhouse for butter and dairy and managed chickens, gardens and orchards. They needed to be skilled or

This account book page records Margaret Brooke's purchases with Caleb Bentley in Sandy Spring. It reflects the careful record-keeping and work of preserving and mending that was done at home. *Courtesy Sandy Spring Museum Archives.*

at least to oversee the drying, pickling and salting to preserve a year-round supply of food.

Custis Lewis's book, unlike Lea's, included only a few recipes for vegetables. As Brandy Schmit pointed out in her editor's introduction, "Vegetable recipes were often neglected in cookbooks because it was assumed that everyone knew how to cook them properly." Of course, Lea was eventually writing for publication and so may have been more thorough in her recording. Potatoes, carrots and radishes were kept layered in sand. Cabbages and cauliflower

Throughout the county, small and well-stocked stores, often located at a crossroads, supplied farm families with the goods they couldn't make for themselves and were a market for local produce. Here, proprietor Arthur Edward Stonestreet poses with his goods and his dog, Tippy. *Courtesy Sandy Spring Museum Archives.*

were layered with straw and buried; corn, peas and beans were dried; onions and garlic were strung and dried. Other vegetables were made into sauces and ketchups or pickled in vinegar. Butter was salted, and eggs were coated in paraffin. Apples were dried or stored, but most fruits were preserved with sugar in jams and preserves or with brandy.

Lea's tested recipes for food and medicine are, as Weaver noted, a record of "regionalities," being for example, "one of the first American cookbook authors to publish a recipe for scrapple." Dishes such as apple butter, bacon dumplings and bologna reflect a Pennsylvania Dutch influence. The produce of the county's orchards was preserved as apple butter or cider "cheese," following German tradition, made with less sugar than jams and spiced with fennel seed, ground cloves and nutmeg. Another option was peaches preserved in cider, and Lea mentioned local fox grapes and raccoon grapes as good for jam and jelly.

In the English pie tradition, Lea offered pot pie made by lining a Dutch oven with pastry and covering the stew inside with a pastry lid, which Woys Weaver called a folk variant of more elaborate standing pies. She also included a recipe for rusks, a faintly sweet biscuit that could be eaten fresh from the oven or stored until dried and crisp, a long-standing method of preserving bread, from ancient Greek *paximadia*, soldier's hardtack and English ship's biscuit.

The Quaker temperance tradition meant that Lea's recipes for Blackberry Cordial, Ginger Wine and Rose Brandy were meant for medicinal use or flavoring cakes. The community's teetotalling entertainments revolved around cakes, biscuits and ice creams. Weaver postulated that the book's southern recipes can be traced to her son-in-law, Henry Stabler, son of Edward Stabler, whose Alexandria apothecary served George Washington and is now a historic site on Fairfax Avenue. From American Indians, Lea gathered recipes for squash, terrapin and green corn, and from Africans, recipes for okra and gumbo. As Weaver wrote, "Everyone sat at the table."

As one might expect from a Quaker who didn't own slaves, Lea seems willing to take on more work herself. "Do with as few domestics as possible; assist with the work yourself," she advised. Lea's advice in dealing with servants is to encourage them—leaving time for the women to take care

"Sandy Spring can get up more occasions for fried chicken than any place I ever saw." In 1969, the Women's Board of the Montgomery General Hospital served fried chicken to hundreds of diners at its annual fundraising supper and bazaar. *Courtesy Women's Board Medstar Montgomery Medical Center, Olney, MD.*

of their own clothes, to read and to knit. Much of her advice would sound familiar to a contemporary manager—give workers time for "rest and recreation" and they will return "renewed in health and spirits." Judging from her advice, Lea's homestead—where she encouraged charity, valued work, served punctual meals and taught children to preside graciously over the table—was one of order and calm.

After Lea's death in 1858 from a protracted illness, the cookbook went out of print, unmentioned even in her obituary. She had been eclipsed by Lydia Marie Child, who though not a Quaker wrote on morality, abolition and cookery in ways that appealed to Quakers. As food became even more linked with morality through the writings of Mary Mann, who advocated eating grains and vegetables, and the health efforts of Sylvester Graham, Elizabeth Lea's heavy farm food would come to be seen as old-fashioned and out of step with the fashion for scientific cookery.

Likewise, farm operations modernized. Gasoline and steam power would replace water and horsepower, with 1870s threshers operated by steam by 1904. It would be the same transition for harvesters, wire and twine binders and the use of silos in the 1880s, mechanized milk separators in the 1890s and incubators and brooders in 1900. Mills as well would shift away from water power and eventually be replaced by the large farms and industrial-scale production in the Midwest.

More Useful Part of Household Duties—Maryland Corn Cakes

"If you wish to have an early breakfast, make every preparation that you can, over night; set the table, have the relish cut, ready to cook, or to warm over—and cold bread may be sliced, and wrapped in a cloth to keep it moist. Coffee should be ground, and dry fuel, and water at hand. With these preparations, breakfast may be ready in half an hour from the time the fire is made. If you have warm corn bread, or rolls, it will require more time; but if you have them made up over night, and put in a cool place, they will not sour, and can soon be baked. Maryland biscuit are very convenient, as they are always ready, and will keep good a week. I have found it a great advantage to set the table over night, particularly if you have a separate room to eat in; although it takes but a short time, every minute is important in the morning."

Lea's sensible advice for a calm morning rings true today, but in early kitchens, breakfast was far more complicated than a slice of bread in the toaster. In Domestic Cookery, she spends nearly two pages on how to make yeast using corn flour, potatoes or milk, and in recipes for Egg Rolls, French Rolls or Superior Boiled Milk Rolls, she calls for "half a tea-cup of good yeast." Even her quick breads, like muffins, call for yeast, since chemical leaveners—baking powder or soda—weren't commercially available. Her recipe for Maryland Corn Cakes is somewhere between a crepe and a pancake, cooked on a properly hot griddle and served promptly.

Mix a pint of corn meal with rich milk, a little salt and an egg; it should be well beaten with a spoon and made thin enough to pour on the iron; take in cakes the size of a breakfast plate; butter and send them hot to the table.

Our modern interpretation is a bit richer, and if you like, you can add ¼ teaspoon of baking powder for a lighter cake.

1 cup cornmeal
¼ teaspoon salt
1 ¼ to 1 ½ cups whole milk
1 large egg
Melted butter to cook
Syrup or jam to serve

Whisk together the cornmeal and salt.

Stir enough milk into the cornmeal to make a pourable batter, whisking to break up any lumps. Whisk in the egg.

Heat your griddle or cast-iron skillet until a drop of water sizzles; oil or butter the surface, and pour out the batter to the size of a saucer.

Cook until the cakes stiffen and their edges are lightly brown. Flip the cakes, cook a few more minutes and serve hot with syrup or jam.

Chapter 5

WAR, FOOD AND POWER

*L*and and geography shaped Montgomery County's history, and of course, geography would shape its Civil War experience. The county's location across the Potomac River from the Confederate state of Virginia, with the C&O Canal on its western border, a distance of only forty miles to the free state of Pennsylvania and a day's ride from the capital city, made the county a target and crossroads for mustering armies.

Although not the scene of any Civil War battles, the county roiled during this period. The Underground Railroad stitched its way through farmhouse cellars and stream valleys, Union and Confederate causes tore apart neighbors and families and the county's roads, farms and canals were targeted by troops on both sides. Food was an important feature of economy, power and survival.

By virtue of their location, many Montgomery County residents had close family and commercial ties to Virginia. There were a number of ferry crossings, and families owned land and farm operations on both sides of the river. Many county residents owned slaves and were Southern sympathizers. One of those Confederate supporters was Elijah Viers White, who grew up in Poolesville and later bought a farm across the Potomac in Loudoun County, Virginia. He was an example of the close ties of trade, transportation and family that wove throughout the region—who was a friend and who was an enemy would shift with every bend in the road.

White captured three hundred troops in the 1861 Battle of Ball's Bluff, across the Potomac in Loudoun County. He'd later buy and operate Conrad's

Ferry, renamed White's Ferry. His Civil War service is commemorated in a stained-glass window, across the Potomac, in St. James's Episcopal Church in Leesburg and in Boyd's *History of Montgomery County*: "Among the officers in the Confederate service, none were more distinguished for capacity, efficiency and valor, than the lamented Colonel Ridgely Brown, Colonel Elijah Viers White, Colonel T.H.S. Boyd, Colonel Gus Dorsey and Colonel Benjamin White…all of revolutionary descent, and who, whether in a good or bad cause, illustrated the valor of the race and well maintained the reputation of the old Maryland Line." Boyd was writing in 1879, after the war had been fought, but clearly the issues of agency and power had not been resolved.

Maryland itself harbored the North and South—the state never seceded, but neither did it vote for Lincoln. In Montgomery County, Lincoln won with just 55 percent of the votes in 1860 and just 25 percent of the county's votes in 1864. In 1863, the Emancipation Proclamation only applied to states that had seceded, and Maryland didn't make slavery illegal until a year later. Some of the county's eighteen thousand residents were slaveholders who supported the Union, others were slaveholders who supported the Confederacy and still others were anti-war Quakers who'd freed their enslaved workers decades before. One-fourth of county residents were Black, and one-third of those were free. With a sympathizer population and at a critical border, Maryland was placed under martial law, which allowed searches without a warrant, jail without a trial and property seizure.

In 1928, the Montgomery County Agricultural Society marked its Diamond Jubilee and recounted a history of the fair. It was held continuously since 1846, except for "a few stormy years during the Civil War when the site of the fairgrounds was occupied by Union troops and when many of the society leaders were away fighting under the banners of the South or North. The membership of the society was divided over the right and wrong of the great conflict." Francis Preston Blair of Silver Spring, a member of Lincoln's administration, was removed from membership due to his antislavery activities. A resolution pointed out "that a majority of the members were slave owners and 'as such vitally interested in enforcing and sustaining all laws passed under the authority of the Constitution of the United States for the protection of their rights and property.'"

Some farms welcomed troops. In *Montgomery County: A Pictorial History*, the authors recount that in early September 1862, the Army of Northern Virginia crossed the Potomac at White's Ford and mustered more than thirty thousand men in Maryland. Officers, including Colonel White and his

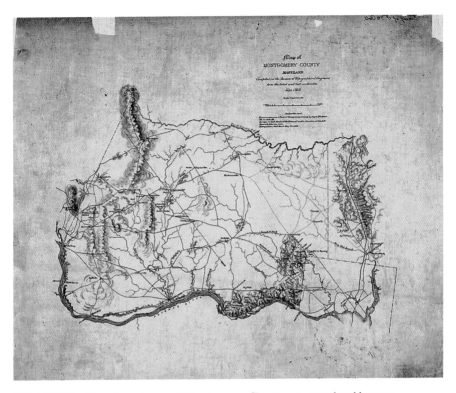

This 1862 War Department map of Montgomery County was completed by army engineers, who included rail lines, roads, bridges and waterways and the topography of cliffs along the Potomac River that would become lookout points. *Courtesy National Archives.*

commander, Stonewall Jackson, "went to Dickerson for dinner, followed by their men. White's mother-in-law, Mary Elizabeth Trundle Gott, collected her friends and prepared ham, fried chicken, potatoes, corn, squash, and blackberry pie for the sudden but welcome guests."

Some farms became military encampments, and most found their produce requisitioned, or plundered, depending on where your sympathies lay. Boyd wrote, "[T]he business of farming was, in many localities, suspended. Houses and fences were destroyed, and farms laid waste by the marching and counter-marching of armies and the general ravages of war." While encamped troops provided county farms with a ready market for milk and prepared foods, the farms were also targets for pilfered chickens and apples. As William Offutt noted in *Bethesda: A Social History*, "Tombstones became oven walls, and fences fed campfires."

For some in the county, the war could be treated as a distant thing. *The Annals of Sandy Spring* recorded the rare sight of "[a] small troop of cavalry, wearing the gray uniform, which we had hitherto only read of…along the roads leading through the centre of this our own neighborhood." For those who'd hidden their horses from the troops, this passage was described as "a mere ripple," but the war would come closer with the sound of cannon fire and fleeing men and horses from the Battle of New Market, an event that suspended business and required more hiding of horses.

In *Memories of Eighty Years*, Mary Coffin Brooke recalled that their home in Sandy Spring, Fair Hill, was "an old house and often the cannonading on the upper Potomac, or even firing in platoons in practice, would rattle the windows with a suddenness that was a little hard on one's nerves, especially as it was necessary to maintain an appearance of composure." When the war came closer, Sandy Spring Quakers proved their loyalty by supplying the sick and wounded with clothing and food.

Food was supplied, quite literally, on the hoof. Brooke noted, "When droves of beef cattle were driven past the house, on their way to our neighboring farmers to be fattened for the army, the bellowing of the cattle, the galloping of the twenty horsemen in charge, and the barking of a score of dogs bringing in strays, made a pandemonium that rendered sleep impossible."

For others, the war was even closer and more than just noise. In Dawsonville, Union forces trampled fields and fences. In 1864, John DeSellum put up Jubal Early and his staff at Summit Hall after the Battle of Monocacy and took the opportunity to make his arguments against secession during dinner, as well as recount his losses in horses, crops and fences due to the Rebel army.

In Poolesville, Philip Johnson, a former slave interviewed for a WPA project in the late 1930s, recalled, "Yes sah, them Confederates done more things around here than the Yankees did. I remember once during the war they came to town. It was Sunday morning an' I was sittin' in the gallery of the ole brick Methodist Church. One of them came to de door and he pointed his pistol right at that preacher's head." Johnson continued by describing how he had to run and hide to avoid the soldiers.

In his book *Civil War Guide to Montgomery County, Maryland*, Charles T. Jacobs recorded various claims for damages. Samuel Magruder, whose land had been used by the signal corps as a lookout point, sought $3,306 for damages from the federal government. Nathan Allnutt's 150 acres at Great Seneca Creek was occupied for six weeks by the Union army, and he estimated it cost him $4,100 for loss of use, destruction of crops and his fence rails used for firewood. George Spates's fence rails were used to build a plank road, and his blacksmith shop was cleaned out of horseshoes, nails and tools. Between

The broad fields at the base of Sugarloaf Mountain were the site of Union army encampments, and its peak was used as a lookout point. *Courtesy Library of Congress.*

1861 and 1865, John DuFief's 400 acres were used as camp and drill sites, and his flour mills, gristmills and sawmills quartered Union troops. And in Silver Spring, Francis Preston Blair's wine cellar and library were looted by Jubal Early's troops in July 1864.

For many Americans, the experience of war has been distant—in other lands and for other people—but the Civil War was fought among families and in neighborhoods. The *Montgomery County Story* recorded Virginia Campbell Moore's recollections of living near Cedar Lane during the Civil War—many of which involve food, sometimes shared freely, sometimes shared under pressure and sometimes simply taken or destroyed. In a 1913 letter to her grandson, she remembered they often fed the Northern soldiers who were stationed at their gate. But one Sunday,

> [w]e *found two officers…sitting on the porch, awaiting us and much to our relief, they only wanted their dinner.…We had a good dinner, fried chicken, etc., and we also had company but there was nothing to do but share it with the self-invited guests, and when those hungry men got through*

This engraving from a sketch image appeared in *Harper's Weekly* in October 1862 showing Union troops at the Battle of South Mountain, with Sugarloaf framing the view. *Courtesy Library of Congress.*

there was a shortage of chicken for the "company." However, they did not suffer for you know our habit of always having cold ham and we wisely checked our hospitality when it reached the frozen custard which was not put on exhibition until the "Yanks" were gone. Perhaps we do not merit the commendation we claim, for our hospitality was somewhat compulsory, it not being wise to antagonize declared enemies backed by the US government.

Later, that same colonel who "had partaken of our hospitality" came to investigate what appeared to be an all-night signal light across the Potomac, but it was just the family sitting up with an ill child. The colonel apologized and retreated, but his men, who resented being called out for nothing, "dashed through the orchard and thrashed off all the fine crop of peaches upon which we were relying to pay for flour at $12.00 per barrel and coffee to replace toasted rye, of both of which we had been destitute for some weeks."

In Silver Spring, Elizabeth Blair Lee seemed to be nearly at the center of wartime Washington political and social life. Her long-established family served in the federal government—her father had been in Andrew Jackson's Kitchen Cabinet, her elder brother was Lincoln's postmaster and her younger brother was a Union general. Her daily letters to her husband, serving as a naval officer, recorded social and political gossip and events. She was a Unionist and repeatedly expresses her frustration with "Sesesh" neighbors, although it seems more like a social frustration than any feeling for the rights of fellow human beings. In response to the possibility of emancipation in Maryland, she wrote, "If I was a large owner of that property [meaning enslaved people] I would put them on wages now and be sure of my crops."

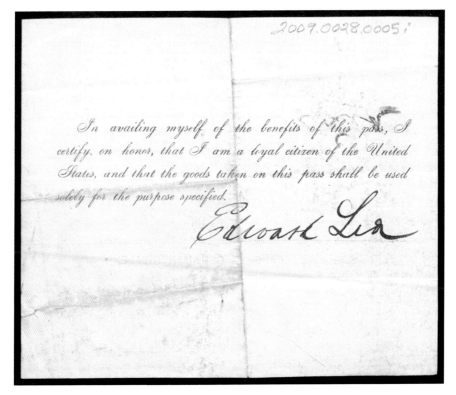

In availing myself of the benefits of this pass, I certify, on honor, that I am a loyal citizen of the United States, and that the goods taken on this pass shall be used solely for the purpose specified.

Edward Lea

Edward Lea was able to obtain this travel pass for himself and a friend to cross "[p]icket lines to their homes in Montgomery County" after his loyalty was vouched for by James Stabler, a clerk in the D.C. Post Office, whose loyalty, was in turn, vouched for by his superintendent, James Kennedy. *Courtesy Sandy Spring Museum Archive.*

Lee's news to her husband recounted her son Blair eating more molasses than is good for him, soldiers helping themselves to chickens and making currant jam for the household. She had the luxury of tending a flower garden, and food production was left to paid and enslaved workers, but she also noted tying up and harvesting asparagus, which she shared with her sister-in-law, and traveling to the family's wheat fields. "Father has done well in farming, he has sold his grass—both growing & cut. Has sold his wheat and made 1,500 dollars which is a great turn out for Silver Spring—he has grazed army beeves—altogether is in great farming feather."

On an 1861 trip to Philadelphia, she observed, "I can not discover anywhere in the North one single sign of hard times—All the manufactures are going….I see no more poor in the streets than usual & wherever I have been I seen nothing but a busy—prosperous people plenty to eat, to wear & to do." That this prosperity is worth noting must make it different than what Lee had seen in Washington. As the war continued, Blair Lee recorded rising food prices, but her household was still able to afford regular deliveries of oysters.

As the war continued to interrupt farming, food became scarce and expensive, especially with a new population of soldiers to feed. The Rockville fairgrounds was a campground and stopping place for Union troops, about fifteen thousand of whom were charged with protecting the C&O Canal and watching for Southern sympathizers. And along with troops came camp followers, who weren't issued rations but rather stole from houses, vegetable gardens, chicken coops and pig pens.

In 1861, a *Philadelphia Inquirer* reporter in Rockville described the county's pattern of settlement—distant farms rather than contained towns: "If anybody need further evidence, let them travel up this way, and be obligated to obtain shelter and refreshment. A pint of milk is only ten cents, and you are surrounded by fields miles away from any facilities for transportation to market. Stop and ask if you can obtain food and shelter for yourself and your horse. Perhaps you are examined from the crown of your hat to the toes of your boots, questioned as to the whys and wherefores of your journey, and then perhaps turned off with 'I don't keep a hotel!'"

The reporter went on to say that the traveler's best bet was to turn himself over to the Union army, although you would have to "be content with a miserable compound called coffee or tea—oh shades of Bohea and Souchong! What tea, fried pork, liverwort, sausage, spare ribs and various other component parts of a hog for breakfast, dinner and tea, and you will not be disappointed." He noted that the endless pork might be stewed, fried, roasted, fricasseed, hashed, minced and more, and cost about two dollars.

Northern soldiers who traveled to Maryland saw a different landscape of farms and towns than they knew. Private Charles Blake was with the Vermont Infantry and wrote to his wife, "[Montgomery County] is one of the finest places I ever saw, great fields of corn and wheat. The wheat is cut, and some is thrashed, and there is great quantities of fruit. There are some apples ripe, but I have had but one.…I should like to live in Maryland." Sadly, Blake was killed in 1864 in the third battle of Winchester. His letter was retrieved by a Confederate soldier.

In his record, *The First Maine Heavy Artillery, 1861–1865: A History of Its Part and Place in the War for the Union, with an Outline of Causes of War and Its Results to Our Country*, Horace H. Shaw recounted observations of the South, the battles the regiment faced, as well as what and how they ate. When they left

Maine, soldiers were told to pack three days of cooked rations, but Shaw noted that in the excitement, "food was not much thought of." They would learn to adapt to the warm climate and camp life, including what to eat to keep themselves from getting sick.

Camp life would call on all the trades, "for soldiers must do many things besides marching, camping, and fighting," including carrying and cooking their food. When camped at Fort Sumner in Bethesda's hills over the Potomac, troops used "straw drawn from the quartermaster, and were soon sleeping on spring beds of their own make with great comfort. They pooled their small capital, bought a cook stove, running the smoke pipe through the top of their Sibley tent, drew their rations uncooked, made a trade with the famous woods cook, Corporal Wing, to cook their food while they did his duty in turn, and were shortly living like nabobs."

As the regiment was deployed into battle, Shaw described sending out foragers to find sustenance for the men and the animals: "They were sent out in squads of ten to twelve men with one or two wagons. Wherever they found a well-filled corncrib it was speedily emptied and the corn loaded into our wagons. Hams, bacon, flour, and all other sorts of provisions were gathered in as well. There seemed to be quite a good supply of apple-jack in the cellar of nearly every plantation house."

At other postings, feeding the troops was a more orderly process: "Issuing rations for a regiment of men is done by the brigade commissary in bulk. For instance, the commissary sergeant of the regiment receives bread, beans, pork, beef, sugar, coffee, salt, soap, and candles, in camp usually three days' rations at a time dealt out to the companies in bulk. Some sergeant of each company, acting as commissary sergeant, receives the rations for his company in bulk. He divides it up to each mess if in camp, and to each man if campaigning."

As Shaw noted, those at the end of the line were left with soup bones, the hard end of bread, the gravelly bits of beans and the "dust of the coffee," but at the mess of a thrifty orderly sergeant, soldiers might dine: "They kept the kettle slowly boiling, had excellent beef stew with dumplings, Scotch broths, meat pie with a crust, good enough for kings, and had plenty left for any growler who called for redress. Our beans baked in the ground were so good, neighboring regiments, who had never learned to cook beans, would sometimes dig them up in the night and so cheat us of our breakfast."

After the war, Alexander Gardner created a "photographic sketchbook" of the war—photos he had taken while working with noted Civil War photographer Mathew Brady. The photos show battlefields and camps but also the architecture of war—forts and headquarters. One plate shows simple tented roof buildings, with piles of barrels outside—the Commissary Department of the Army of the Potomac.

In his accompanying text, Gardner described the stock in glowing terms that not every soldier might agree with: "The Commissary at the General Headquarters of the Army of the Potomac was nothing less than an immense grocery establishment. Coffee, tea, sugar, molasses, bacon, salt pork, fresh beef, potatoes, rice, flour, &c., were always kept on hand in large quantities, and of the best quality."

He also described the disposition of these excellent groceries after the war:

> *It was interesting in the last year of the war to witness the Virginia families flock to Headquarters for the purpose of purchasing supplies of the Commissary. Decrepid* [sic] *men, ladies, children, and family servants crowded the Commissary at stated periods for rations, carrying off their purchased provisions in the oddest vehicles, on horseback, and on foot, some individuals every week walking twenty miles to get their supplies. The provisions sold by the Commissary were disposed of at prices far below market rates, the Government only charging the cost price at wholesale; and as great care was taken in the selection of supplies by the Government agents, it was highly desirable to citizens to purchase rations. This was especially the case with respect to tea, coffee, and sugar, which were bought by the Government in as unadulterated a form as could be found.*

In 1862, Louisa May Alcott came to Georgetown to work in an army hospital. Her observations of hospital administration and operations, as well as the daily of life of nurses and patients, were published in *Commonwealth*, a Boston antislavery newspaper, and later collected into her first book, *Hospital Sketches*.

Alcott observed how much of the day revolved around food. When the trays of bread, meat, soup and coffee appeared, the convalescing soldier transformed from a "dismal ragamuffin into a recumbent hero." As the hospital matron said, "Bless their hearts, why shouldn't they eat? It's their only amusement; so fill every one, and, if there's not enough ready to-night, I'll lend my share to the Lord by giving it to the boys."

As much as the food was rejuvenating, it was still meager. Alcott called the steward "a horn of plenty" but thought the menu could be improved "without plunging the nation madly into debt": "The three meals were 'pretty much of a muchness,' and consisted of beef, evidently put down for the men of '76; pork, just in from the street; army bread, composed of saw-dust and saleratus; butter, salt as if churned by Lot's wife; stewed blackberries, so much like preserved cockroaches, that only those devoid of imagination could partake thereof with relish; coffee, mild and muddy; tea, three dried huckleberry leaves to a quart of water—flavored with lime."

Nevertheless, even this unappealing menu was taken up with enthusiasm, and mealtime caused a stampede. There were no seconds to be had, and if you were late, you went without. Alcott often found herself "dinnerless." She quickly learned her lesson and "that evening went to market, laying in a small stock of crackers, cheese and apples, that my boys might not be neglected, nor myself obliged to bolt solid and liquid dyspepsias, or starve." But her stock didn't last long, "for the rats had their dessert off my cheese, the bugs set up housekeeping in my cracker-bag, and the apples like all worldly riches, took to themselves wings and flew away; whither no man could tell."

In *Hospital Sketches*, Alcott recorded the activity inside and outside the hospital. Georgetown, a busy port town with mills and warehouses, was an important supply depot and store for Union forces. Farms in Montgomery County with a connection to the C&O Canal found a ready market for their produce. Likewise, the canal was a target for Confederate forces. In 1861, Rebel raiding parties crossed from Virginia to destroy locks, break banks and drain water and capture or burn canalboats. In response, between 1862 and 1863, troops were stationed along the canal, including at Edwards Ferry Road, where a depot was established to store and distribute food to Union regiments.

While troop movements and army musters are recorded with pomp and pride, a more stealthy and desperate movement was taking place. Montgomery County is just forty miles from the Pennsylvania border, the first free state above the Mason-Dixon line. This location, and the local sympathetic Quaker community, made the county a route and stop on the Underground Railroad.

The county's enslaved population wasn't as large as in Prince George's County and the Tidewater, where they worked large plantations of labor-intensive crops, particularly tobacco. But it was higher than in Frederick County, a community that worked on smaller farmsteads, manufacturing and mining.

Nonetheless, the county's early land grant plantations grew tobacco, made profitable through the labor of enslaved workers. Growing tobacco is labor-intensive; the crop and product must be tended nearly year-round. In December and January, seeds are set and tended in fertilized beds. From April to June, the seedlings are transplanted in the field and weeded, hoed and picked over to remove flowers—to encourage leaf growth—and the worms that would eat the leaves. The matured leaves are cut in September, before the frost, and the curing, stripping from stems and packaging would take up the next months. It was packed into hogshead barrels, rolled to Georgetown and sold at market.

This high-labor crop led to the neglect of other crops and farm tasks, not supporting a diverse farm economy. Tobacco growing also wasted the soil, and when the market collapsed, farmers turned toward crops like wheat and corn that required less intensive labor. It was a market shift that made it profitable to sell slaves south to work on high-labor cotton plantations. Considered as assets—tools of the economy—rather than as human beings, the treatment of the enslaved population shifted along with the market.

In his 1879 history, Boyd recorded the county's population from the decade of its founding (the last line includes an original mathematical error, but it is unclear which column is incorrect):

Year	White	Colored	Total
1782	10,011	4,407	14,418
1790	11,679	6,324	18,003
1800	8,508	6,550	15,058
1810	9,731	8,249	17,980
1820	9,082	7,318	16,400
1830	12,103	7,713	19,816
1840	8,766	6,690	15,456
1850	9,435	6,425	15,860
1860	11,349	6,973	18,322
1870	13,128	7,434	20,563

Maryland Quakers began to free their slaves before the Revolution. Montgomery County Quakers—including Evan Thomas, Basil Brooke and Thomas Richardson—freed their slaves between 1775 and 1782 and encouraged their neighbors to do the same.

According to Mary Beth Corrigan's research at Georgetown's Tudor Place, "Enslaved and Free African-Americans in Early Nineteenth Century Georgetown," the 1820s were a turning point. With the decline of tobacco, many White farmers moved west, taking slaves with them and breaking family ties. Or, because their land had lost its fertility and thus its value, they sold slaves to finance new ventures.

But other farmers stayed and relied on enslaved labor to work their farms; the relationships can be tracked in newspaper advertisements. From an ad in an 1857 Rockville newspaper: C.J. Maddox offered seventy-five dollars for the return of Charles, "secured in jail so I can get him." In "Enslaved and Free," Corrigan recorded James Allnutt, who owned a farm near Seneca Creek, listing himself in the census as the head of a "family at this time white & black consists of Twenty seven."

With research, we've come to see slavery as a complex network of commercial and family relationships. In Washington, communities of free and enslaved people were related through kinship; many were connected to their owners by blood ties, even though they were treated as capital. This complexity meant that enslaved people were granted different degrees of intimacy and agency by their owners.

In "Enslaved and Free," Corrigan gives name to just a few of these people, using court records, wills and estate lists at Tudor Place, connected to Oakland Farm and the Peter family at Montevideo. In lists of escaped slaves and those handed down through dower and inheritance, she found "Patty, a cook who lived with her husband," and Charles, "a Dining room servant who also was a footman when the carriage was taken out. One night after accompanying the family to Washington, he got drunk and let his coat catch to the wheel. His leg was amputated and [he] later died from complications."

Corrigan also described a labor system that depended on movement. While Black women often worked as domestic servants, Black men moved from fields to farm production to market, depending on the season and plantation. They were able to maintain connections between urban and rural households.

That movement is reflected in Josiah Henson's work at Isaac Riley's three-hundred-acre farm, between 1800 and 1830. Henson's autobiography, *The Life of Josiah Henson, Formerly a Slave, Now an Inhabitant of Canada*, is a valuable first-person resource of an enslaved life and of one in Montgomery County. Today, the Riley Plantation and Henson's story are reconstructed at the site on Old Georgetown Road, where the County Parks Department has undertaken a long-term project to purchase the house and surrounding properties, restore and interpret the buildings and pursue archaeological excavations to understand who lived and worked on the plantation.

Josiah Henson was born in 1789 in Port Tobacco in Charles County, his mother's last child. He recalled that his father was punished for defending his mother against the plantation's overseer—beaten and sold south to Alabama. Henson's remaining family, two brothers and three sisters, were split apart in 1805 when they were sold at auction to settle the estate after the death of his first owner, Dr. Josiah McPherson. With her husband gone and children scattered, Henson's mother was sold to Riley, and Henson was sold to Adam Robb, a Rockville tavern-keeper and neighbor of Riley. The two eventually worked out a trade, and Henson was reunited with his mother on the Riley farm.

Enslaved children began to work at about age five—watching younger siblings, tending animals and helping in the garden or kitchen—and they might be in the fields by age seven. In *Sharp Flashes of Lightning*, Jamie Kuhns recorded life on Riley's

Uncle Tom
BORN IN SLAVERY
ESCAPED TO FREEDOM IN CANADA

In 1849, Josiah Henson published his autobiography as a way to earn money to pay for his brother's freedom. Henson was a leader in his own community; his autobiography made his story and leadership known around the world. *Courtesy Montgomery History.*

farm. He was married to Matilda Middleton, whose brother Francis would eventually come to live with them. For the most part, plantation houses in Montgomery County were not grand, pillared edifices but rather simple farmhouses. The Riley farm had a detached kitchen, and cooking was a valued skill. An enslaved cook fed the family and the laborers and oversaw the garden and the preservation of its produce, although it was unlikely that they had the key to the larder.

Henson's own narrative, paired with recent archaeological excavations, reveals that many of the farm outbuildings supported food production, including slave quarters, a springhouse to keep food cool and hold butter for sale and a slatted corn crib, which allowed air to circulate through dry corn stored on the cob. The dried corn was used for seed or ground into meal. The meat house was where meat, primarily pork, was salted and smoked to preserve it and protect it as a valuable commodity.

The Riley farm also had an apple and peach orchard that supplied fruit, which could also be brewed into cider or brandy. But according to an oral history, the trees were worn out by 1878. The farm's two primary crops were corn and tobacco, but they also grew oats, rye, barley, potatoes and hay.

In his autobiography, Henson described his work on the farm. He was made to "carry buckets of water to the men at work, and to hold a horse-plough, used for weeding between the rows of corn. As I grew older and taller, I was entrusted with the care of master's saddle-horse. Then a hoe was put into my hands and I was soon required to do the day's work of a man; and it was not long before I could do it, at least as well as my associates in misery." He recalled "endless rows of potatoes, which I have hoed so many weary hours."

Henson was acutely aware of the power and relationship between owner and owned, as well as what ownership does to a person. He illustrated that relationship by describing the food allotted to enslaved workers: "The principal food of those upon my master's plantation consisted of corn meal, and salt herrings; to which was added in summer a little buttermilk, and the few vegetables which each might raise for himself and his and his family on the little piece of ground which was assigned to him for the purpose, called a truck patch."

There were two meals a day—breakfast at noon, after a morning's work that started at dawn, and the other when the day's work was finished. Henson's description of food sounds lean but benign when read as a single paragraph. But read in the context of the autobiography—when he is

CORN. This annual grass is called corn in North America and maize elsewhere. Sweet corn was cultivated in the early 1800s and carried into the Ohio Valley by farmers. W.H. Farquhar called corn "that great staple," and culinary historian Susan McLellan Plaisted followed up: "Cornbread was the initial staff of life in America." In *Domestic Cookery*, Elizabeth Ellicott Lea began her chapter on vegetables with corn and a simple recipe "To Boil Green Corn," continuing on with fricassee, fritters and hominy. She used corn flour and hops to make yeast and cornmeal mush to make "good rolls, muffins, flannel cakes, porridge, bannocks, pone, and hoe cake." "To Keep Corn for Winter," cut it off the cob, dry it on plates and hang it in muslin bags.

describing "the provisions for the daily of toil of the slave," a dirt-floor log cabin with less finish than a barn and rudimentary clothing made of "tow cloth," a cheap linen fabric—the element of control and a lack of the joy or generosity we associate with food are evident.

Henson underlined the fact, pointing out "the needless misery" created by a man in a position to tyrannize: "[H]is slaves had little opportunity for relaxation from wearying labor…supplied with the scantiest means of sustaining their toil by necessary food."

It is not surprising that Henson recorded that he "helped them to some of the comforts they were denied by him who owned them: Meat was not part of our regular food; but my master had plenty of sheep and pigs, and sometimes I have picked out the best one I could find in the flock, or the drove, carried it a mile or two into the woods, slaughtered it, cut it up, and distributed among the poor creatures, to who, it was at once food, luxury, and medicine." He "esteemed it among the best" of his deeds.

Henson is describing food as power—by successfully farming and marketing the farm's produce, he has a significant impact on the household economy; Riley came to depend on him. But Henson was still limited in that his work might benefit him in the short run, making his life and his family's more comfortable, but he couldn't guarantee that his family would stay intact, let alone earn equity, establish his own farm or leave an inheritance. He was subject to beatings and punishment from his master, as well as from any White person in the community. Henson's attempt to learn to read was quashed early on, and later in life, when he did learn to read and write, the first letters he wrote were his master's initials, I and R, copied from the butter mold.

Another manifestation of food as power is Henson's account of feeding his mistress's brother, who lived on the farm. "Francis…who used to complain… of the meanness of the household; and he would often come to me, with tears in his eyes, to tell me he could not get enough to eat. I made him my friend for life, by sympathizing with his emotions, and satisfying his appetite, sharing with him the food I took care to provide for my own family." Francis would later speak for Henson, moving him a few steps closer to freedom.

Through his work and alliances with enslaved workers built partially through food, Henson gained his owner's trust and acted as the farm's superintendent. Using Henson as superintendent saved Riley the expense of paying a white overseer, and Henson's knowledge of the farm and its workers increased the crop output. He also took the crops to market, where he "did sell it for better prices than anyone else he could employ."

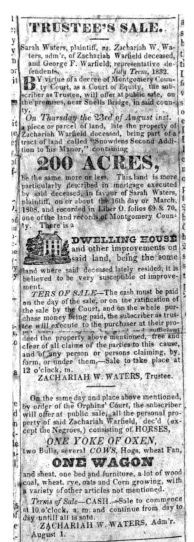

The advertisement from an 1832 issue of the *Maryland Free Press* is for the sale of the estate of Zachariah Warfield, the house and land, and separately "all the personal property (except the Negroes)," making it brutally clear that enslaved people had little to no agency over their bodies and lives and were treated as property. *Courtesy Montgomery History.*

In the position of superintendent, Henson gained some control, overseeing the plantation's daily life and operations, as well as the implicit and explicit trade of labor, freedom and food. But is it possible to cheat a person who owns you? "I will not deny that I used his property more freely than he would have done himself, in supplying his people with better food; but if I cheated him in this way, in small matters, it was unequivocally for his own benefit in more important ones."

As overseer, Henson was resourceful and dependable; meanwhile, Riley, from his own incompetence and the lawsuits against him, was close to bankruptcy, at risk of losing all his assets—home, land and slaves. As Henson wrote, "The poor, drinking, furious, shiftless, moaning creature was utterly incapable of managing his affairs."

Before the sheriff could seize his property—land, machinery, crops, livestock and enslaved people—Riley decided to send his slaves, led by Henson, to his brother's plantation in Kentucky. Henson led his family and eighteen others on a thousand-mile journey, in the winter—daunting but better than being sold and split apart. They traveled through Virginia, West Virginia and through the mountains; when questioned, Henson showed his travel pass. Despite the temptation to end the journey in Ohio, where they could live free, the party continued. It was a decision Henson would come to regret when Riley sent word to sell his slaves and return to Maryland with the money.

Henson spent three years in Kentucky, where he found the "farm was larger and more fertile, and there was a greater abundance of food, which is, of course, one of the principal sources of the comfort of a slave, debarred, as he is, from so many enjoyments which other men can obtain."

Upon returning to Maryland, Henson sought to buy his freedom, but Isaac Riley was loath to lose the value that Henson brought. Henson called on Francis, Riley's brother-in-law whom he had once fed, for help, and Francis negotiated a deal that would allow Henson to return to Kentucky to his family. But when Riley cheated him out of his manumission papers, Henson determined that he would escape.

In *The Underground Railroad in Montgomery County*, Anthony Cohen traced the "organized system of escape through the County," pointing out that this system began before the Civil War. On one side, newspaper ads offered rewards for escaped slaves. In 1789, William Smith of Seneca offered a reward of five pounds for the return of Bachelor, Thomas Johns of Newport-Mill offered twenty dollars for a mulatto man named Bob and Thomas Beall offered three dollars for the return of a "mulatto wench" who ran away near the Montgomery County Courthouse on July 4.

On the other side, the Sandy Spring Quaker community questioned "the authority of man in the keeping of other men as slaves." Their actions—manumitting slaves and donating land for a place of worship—followed their faith, and they sometimes violated the law to help fugitive slaves make connections with northern Quaker communities willing to support the Underground Railroad.

Before the 1850 Fugitive Slave Law, the Pennsylvania border, forty miles away—a few days' walk—was a gateway to freedom, but it still required a network of helpers to guide and support freedom seekers. Fugitives had to evade patrols that monitored the county highways. When an armed party of forty Black travelers was spotted within two miles of the Frederick Road, near Rockville, the Montgomery Volunteers were called out in pursuit.

Unlike open roads, streams and rivers provided somewhat secluded routes, and there are recollections of borrowed shawls, cryptic notes, lamps in windows and houses with "a very unnecessary number of cellars." Caleb Bentley's home in Sandy Spring, which came to be known as Madison House after hosting the runaway president in the face of British aggression, has a hidden room "behind the wall of an existing cellar." As Cohen noted, all are clues to the Underground Railroad in Montgomery County.

Henson's path was different. In sermons and church gatherings, he heard calls for the abolition of slavery, and after Riley's treachery, Henson determined to escape from bondage in Kentucky. He gathered his family and enough provisions for a two-week journey, by foot at night, to Cincinnati. He wrote that "a day or two previous to getting there, our provisions were used up, and I had the misery to hear the cry of hunger and exhaustion from those I loved so dearly." He dared to move during the day to find food. "I approached the first house I saw, and asked if they would sell me a little bread and meat. No, they had nothing for black fellows." He finally found someone who was willing to sell, but "who wanted to see how little he could give me for my quarter of a dollar." Hunger eased, they traveled on, but through wilderness unable to be provisioned, relying on a few mouthfuls each of dried beef.

In 1830, Henson and his family made it to Canada, where he established a Black community, worked sometimes for wages and sometimes for shares and came to procure some pigs, a cow and a horse. Henson wrote his autobiography to earn money to manumit his brother, John, but the book would also make him a strong voice in the abolition movement. He earned a "harvest that will ripen only in eternity."

After the Civil War, some Black families chose to stay in Montgomery County, near family and community, on land they knew. One community was long established in Sandy Spring, where Quaker farmers had begun in the late 1700s to free the enslaved people they held. The Sharp Street Church was the center of this community, as described in a circa 1899 Department of Labor Bulletin: "Here within a stone's throw, as it were, of the seat of government is a thriving agricultural community, among whom live still the descendants of Negro families which have been free for a century and a quarter. It is this exceptional fact of a long-continued free existence in the midst of surrounding slavery which seems to warrant the special investigation of the Negroes of Sandy Spring in order to see what are the social and economic results to them of their opportunities during several generations as freemen. The better to understand the local conditions, a brief sketch of both county and neighborhood is desirable."

The demographic study was modeled on one undertaken by W.E.B. Du Bois of Farmville, Virginia, and both recorded the family compositions, their housing and education and the work they do. Du Bois observed that on a single look, a community may look industrious or lazy and emphasized the importance of accurate observations and data, rather than anecdote or single incident to understand a society. "These apparently contradictory statements made continually of Negro groups all over the land are both true to a degree, and become mischievous and misleading only when stated with reservation as true of a whole community."

The Sandy Spring community included owners, renters and farmhands occupying as tenants. While some women worked as domestics, many of them worked at their own homes. While the White and Black communities worked together, it wasn't without conflict. As the report's author noted, "[D]omestic service is, economically speaking, one of the two sources of the growing race alienation, the other being political—the one affecting primarily the women, the other affecting primarily the men."

While the work and prosperity varied, over time, the Black families were able to achieve some prosperity. "It must be remembered that a great many of these Sandy Spring families have gardens and fowls, that many own a horse, and that the farmers among them have cows and all the usual farm supplies for their family needs."

Across the county, in 1890, Black people formed one-third of the population, mostly living in freedmen's communities established throughout the county, on land purchased from former owners, including Tobytown, Scotland and Sugarland. Gwen Hebron Reese's work with the Sugarland Ethno-History Project has documented the community's history and life; her great-grandfather Patrick Hebron was one of the community's founders. It was formed in the 1870s and 1880s, near Poolesville, when freed slaves purchased land from White landowners, including Jane Pleasants, George Dawson and the Allnutts.

Sugarland grew to include about forty families who worked as farmers, blacksmiths, teachers and carpenters, as well as at the Seneca Quarry. Others worked as farmhands and domestics, and some were "hucksters" who drove market wagons, picking up and selling farm and finished goods— eggs, a spool of thread and so on—in spread-out rural communities. Among them was one of the community's founders, Isaac Bell, who ran the local store, which he stocked (from weekly trips to Frederick) with meat, sugar and flour, as well as candy and ice cream. But the community's first store, in the 1880s, was operated by a White merchant. As pointed out in the Sugarland history *I Have Started for Canaan*, while they were no longer enslaved, Black people didn't have access to the required financing.

The freedmen's communities were centered on three buildings—church, school and community hall—which were financed and built by community members. Each family had a garden and grew crops and produce for sale and for their own use. Heritage Montgomery's *African-American Heritage Cookbook* described how farmers preserved their produce—a technique used by White farmers as well: "Families living in houses without a cellar stored potatoes in 'potato holes' or 'preserving kilns.' Arnold and Joe

Basil Dorsey and his wife, Nancy Beckwith Dorsey, began building their house in Sugarland in 1874. Although only foundations remain, an archaeological dig sponsored by the Sugarland Ethno-History Project and Montgomery College uncovered numerous household and farming tools, including fork handles, a stoneware jug and a patent medicine bottle. *Courtesy Sugarland Ethno-History Project, photograph by Catie Leonard.*

Hawkins from Purdum say that such kilns were made by digging a hole in the ground below the frost line, covering the bottom with straw, and adding the potatoes or other tuber vegetables such as turnips and parsnips or firm fruits such as apples or pears. Only one type of vegetable or fruit was put in each kiln. It was then covered with straw and a mound of dirt, and a circle was dug around it to keep the water from it."

Basil Dorsey and Nancy Beckwith Dorsey bought their land in 1871 and moved into their small home with their five children in 1874. Although that house is gone, recent archaeological work on the site, a project of the Sugarland Ethno-History Project with the help of Montgomery College, has found evidence of their lives. A canning jar, a tool to stoke the fire, a medicine bottle and a tractor blade speak of life in the home and on the farm.

In one of the oral histories collected by Hebron Reese, Suzanne Johnson, the great-granddaughter of Samuel Lee, the patriarch of one of the community's founding families, spent summers and holidays in Sugarland. She recalled her grandfather's property—a small frame house, "a smoke house, root cellar, chicken coop and storage shed. There was a vegetable garden to the left of the lane that went up to the house, and one down past the chicken coop. There was a pen where he raised hogs. And there was an 'out house.'" The food produced on his small farm was memorable:

> *Every November, Granddaddy would slaughter hogs. He would send us in the house while they killed the hogs. When we saw them again, they were cleaned and ready to be cut up. That was an education. I learned where the cuts of pork come from. Killing hogs was an "all weekend affair." Everybody had a job to do. The men cut up the hogs into chops, hams, ribs, bacon, etc. We cut up the fat for lard, ground the meat for the sausage, and cleaned out the casing for the sausage. And then we ate! Aunt Bessie [Bessie Lee] would flour and fry slices of fresh ham and fry some apples! My grandfather would "sugar cure" the hams himself. He would season them and hang them in the smokehouse. Every time I eat a sugar-cured ham, I think of him.*

All the families had gardens and shared seasonal work. An oral history collected by Hebron Reese includes Mary Beckwith's recollections:

> *All the children played a role in the gathering of food for canning by the adults…[they] would participate in gathering apples for applesauce and apple butter. They would fill large bags with apples and take them to the adults to be prepared. Everyone helped in the canning project. The women would peel the apples and prepare them for cooking. They would bring jars, all different sizes, to use for canning. No matter how many jars you brought, the proceeds were divided equally among the families. The men prepared breakfast while the women worked on the apples. The children had the job of stirring the apples, as they were cooking so that they would not stick or burn. The same process took place when it was time to pick berries, peaches and vegetables.*

These were segregated communities, with separate schools, churches, stores and community events. Even in Sandy Spring, where Quakers had freed slaves beginning in the late 1700s, Black schools were supported but separate. Washington Grove hosted camp meetings for White churches, while Emory Grove was the site for Black church camp meetings. School segregation would continue into the 1950s; many new suburban communities would be built with restrictive covenants. Ginger Hoffacker recalled that her aunt and uncle's restaurant, Staub's, operated as many did:

> *An older black man named Lawrence…worked for my aunt and uncle for years. Lawrence would always stock the bottled drinks in the built-in refrigerators for all the customers and take care of any cleanup and maintenance that needed to be done. The sad part was there was a room between where the western wear was sold and the restaurant's side door where Lawrence had set up chairs and stools and where Black people would eat, instead of in the adjacent restaurant. It seemed normal because that was the way things were back in those days and thankfully we have changed!*

Religious "camp meetings" took place in August, what Martha Sprigg Poole called the "farmer's vacation," when crops are well planted but

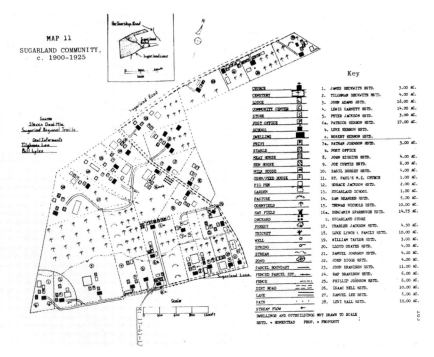

Sugarland was established as a freedmen's community, and this sketch—based on oral histories, deed research and archaeology—shows how homes strove to be self-sufficient, with land that held gardens, orchards, hen houses and other outbuildings that would support a family with food. *Courtesy Maryland Historical Trust, created by George McDaniel, Sugarloaf Regional Trails.*

CATAWBA GRAPE. In *History of Western Maryland*, Scharf wrote, "In the garden of Mr. Scholl, at the east end of town [Clarksburg], the celebrated Catawba grape, which has since gained such a world-wide reputation, was probably first cultivated in America." He noted that pomologists were still making pilgrimages to Scholl's garden. The grape's reputation came when it left the county and was taken up by German settlers, particularly in Cincinnati, to make Hock, a lightly sweet white wine. Catawbas, unlike most grapes native to North America, didn't impart a musky flavor and aroma to the wine.

before the all-consuming harvest. They were clearly social occasions. The *Montgomery County Story* described an 1870 camp meeting at Emory Grove: "Food was always an intrinsic part of camp. Large black kettles of golden cabbage, ears of corn, and potatoes over open fires sent enticing aromas through the campgrounds. Ham and fried chicken were a must. Thick slices of cake, pie, and ice cream added an extra joy to the meal. On the other hand, large numbers of families prepared their lunch or dinner at home and enjoyed eating under the numerous shade trees."

In October 1909, the Negro Agricultural Fair in Sandy Spring attracted Black farmers from around the state to this largest and most established settlement of freedmen. The free Black community in Sandy Spring was established in 1822, setting up a church on land deeded in 1854—the Sharp Street Methodist Church (named for the mother church of Black Methodism in Baltimore), which also functioned as a school and the center for numerous community events, including fairs, revivals, rummage sales, sewing schools and debating and musical clubs.

In 1881, there were twenty-three Black schools in the county, and by 1893, there were thirty-three, but one in five Black residents was illiterate. Education focused on trades, following the model proposed by Booker T. Washington. By 1909, the Maryland Normal and Agricultural Institute in Sandy Spring had 177 students and five faculty who taught agricultural, manual, household skills and teacher training.

On October 11, 1900, Sandy Spring's Black residents celebrated with a procession from Olney to Ashton and back again to mark the thirtieth anniversary of the passage of the Fifteenth Amendment. Horse-drawn floats displayed the skills of the Black tradesmen and women—carpenters, blacksmiths, farmers and seamstresses—who contributed to the area's economy, and the community's brass bands marched alongside.

In *The Annals of Sandy Spring*, W.H. Farquhar noted his community's joy at the end of the Civil War and its mourning for the assassinated president. The seasons continued to turn, and farmers celebrated spring and hoped for promising yields. Unfortunately, "The important crop of wheat, which had been declining in our neighborhood for several years, reached what is to be hoped will be the lowest point of production....The apple, most valuable of fruits, was also a remarkable failure." Nonetheless, the recently established Horticultural Society held a display of garden vegetables, corn and seasonal fruit in the Lyceum building, described as a "very creditable affair."

Scharf described the period after the Civil War in Montgomery County as "the free labor period" and touted the improvements and expansions made to buildings, fences, churches and schools. The Metropolitan Branch of the B&O Railroad delivered lime, bone phosphates and other fertilizers, which led to an increased production of corn and wheat, fed to "at least twenty-five mills, located on the various streams in the county, several of which are merchant-mills." He continued: "Market-gardening and fruit-growing, too, are becoming extensive industries here, and can nowhere else be more successfully prosecuted, the soil yielding abundantly and of the best quality all the vegetables and fruits common to a temperate climate. Wine production is also growing into quite a business, and cannot fail to prove successful, as this county is the home of many varieties of the wild grape and the native soil of the Catawba. These various industries must soon place the people in the very van of agricultural progress."

And although there was renewed investment in farming and the techniques, production and transportation that support it, farmers would shift to serve a growing urban population, and county land would increasingly take its value from development as farmland was turned into suburban, streetcar-connected house lots.

The Hard Work of Making an Icon—Maryland Beaten Biscuits

Recipes for Maryland beaten biscuits or beat biscuits are often brief, assuming the cook knows the technique and the desired result. Maria Watkins's recipe from the Up-to-Date Cookbook *instructs to "beat three quarters of an hour"; other vintage recipes make the picturesque recommendation to beat the dough with an axe handle and recommend 20 minutes of beating for family, 30 minutes for company. Who did all that beating? Likely enslaved cooks.*

Some of those enslaved stayed in Montgomery County and founded communities like Sugarland, where Gwen Hebron Reese grew up as a descendant of one of the founding families. In an oral history, Reese and other descendants shared recollections of growing up in Sugarland. Many of their fondest memories are of food—sweets, seasonal treats and family traditions. Hebron Reese recalled that "[a] trip to grandmother's meant a fresh baked homemade roll beaming with butter or a taste of a simple baked cake. She lived two houses across the fields and in full view of our kitchen so we knew Mom was keeping a watchful eye on us. Aunt Bessie was noted for homemade pies and cakes so we anticipated sweets when sent to her house. She lived about a half a mile from us."

The southern biscuits we think of are fluffy, floury clouds and the technique of beating a stiff dough seems counterintuitive to creating a tender crumb. Think of beat biscuits as a type of cracker—crispy and puffed hollow with air. The dry result is in the tradition of ship's biscuit; they will keep.

Beat Biscuits
To one quart flour add one teaspoonful salt, half teacup lard and enough cold water to make very stiff dough; beat three quarters of an hour and bake not too fast. One quart flour will make about forty biscuits.
Mrs. Watkins

Mrs. Watkins doesn't offer a lot of guiding information; how much is a half teacup and what is the time and temperature of "not too fast"? Even our contemporary version will require some practice, just like fluffy biscuits, until you come to instinctively know the proper texture and cooking time. You can choose to dock them or not by poking holes with a fork and use your own preference of fat—butter or bacon fat—although some cooks swear by lard. As for technique, folding the dough as you beat it will create layers that separate in the oven. For time and temperature, different recipes make different recommendations. Some bake quickly at 500°F, others at a low 200°F and leave the biscuits to dry and crisp in a warm oven. Most likely, it's a matter of your pans, your arm and your oven, but you can start with the interpretation here.

2 cups flour
½ teaspoon salt
¼ cup lard, bacon fat, butter (or a mixture of)
⅔ cup cold water

Stir together the flour and salt and then cut in the fat using a pastry cutter or fork until the fat is distributed through the flour. Start by adding ⅓ cup of water, adding a spoonful at a time to draw the dough together.

Gather the dough into a disc and beat it with a rolling pin or meat tenderizer (or even the more traditional axe handle) for about 45 minutes. As it flattens, fold the dough in half and keep beating. With more beating, the dough will become silky and elastic.

Roll the dough to about ⅛-inch thick and cut into rounds. Bake them on a cookie sheet at 400°F for about 15 minutes, until the biscuits are puffed but not quite brown.

Chapter 6

FARMING IN THE CAPITAL REGION

fter the Civil War and through a period of increasing industrialization, many in Montgomery County returned to farming. But with a postwar boom, down-county communities shifted from farming to suburban development connected by streetcar lines to well-paid, reliable federal government jobs. Remaining farms also shifted their production—many from wheat to dairy—to meet local demand. How families fed themselves changed as well, and seasonal farm life would begin to fade as the county became more suburban.

In 1850, the land plat called "No Gain" along Brookville Road in Chevy Chase was described in the U.S. Agricultural Census. William S. Allison held one hundred improved acres and forty unimproved acres with farming equipment worth $500. His five horses, eight milk cows, three other cattle, ten sheep and ten swine were worth $700. He had slaughtered animals worth another $20. Farm products consisted of 300 bushels of wheat, 15 bushels of rye, 375 bushels of Indian corn, 200 bushels of oats, 300 bushels of Irish potatoes, 15 tons of hay, 40 pounds of wool and 250 pounds of butter. As William LeoGrande pointed out in his research for the *Montgomery County Story*, this was not a gentry holding, but a farm large enough to support a family.

Allison sold the farm in 1853 to Samuel Anderson in 1860, valued at $13,000, but by 1870, it was valued at only $7,000. LeoGrande noted that Anderson could no longer use enslaved labor and was paying wages including board of $1,200 per year. He was still producing the same crops—potatoes, hay, corn and winter wheat—but his butter production increased and he butchered more animals, for which there would have been a ready market in the growing city of Washington. This farm had been part of larger land grants and planted with tobacco, but it would be gone by 1890, replaced by suburban subdivision into the community of Chevy Chase.

Operating by 1873, the B&O Railroad's Metropolitan Branch cut diagonally across the county from Takoma Park northwest to Dickerson, running two passenger and two freight trains each day, increasing in number every year. The line supported developing suburbs, connected farmers to markets in Washington and quickly and inexpensively delivered farm supplies, including fertilizer, from the port in Baltimore. It also raised prices of land along the rail line, making it more attractive to develop land than to farm it.

Carroll Duvall grew up in Kensington on land his family had been granted in 1652. In an oral history, he recalled that his grandfather Charles was likely a farmer and that his father, George, was a builder and contractor of houses in Kensington and Chevy Chase. Carroll worked for forty-four years for the federal government in the Forest Service and the Department of Agriculture. It's an employment evolution that almost perfectly reflects the county's history, from farming to suburban development to government employment.

In 1900, Duvall was twelve years old, and Kensington was a small place—about 250 homes, dirt streets and brick sidewalks. Mr. Hopkins ran the grocery store that he started in the old town hall building. Duvall called it a general store: "He would send a man around in a horse and buggy who would take your orders in the morning and in the afternoon would deliver it. On Saturday night you went down and paid your bill."

The train made life in Kensington convenient. Duvall recalled: "The train service on the B&O was excellent. You could go to town and back almost anytime you wanted." Soon enough car ownership became more widespread. He remembered that a group of local men christened their new cars with bottles of ginger ale from the Trowbridge Pharmacy.

Nonetheless, in the early 1900s, Montgomery County was still a mostly rural place. The census that year counted a total population of 30,451, with 26,696 living in a "rural area." Most residents earned their living from farming, and 85 percent of the county's land was farmland.

In fact, even Bethesda was rural enough to accommodate a federal Animal Disease Research Station in 1897, and in 1910, an expanded Bethesda facility was working on swine plague and pneumonia in cattle,

ADVERTISING TO A CHANGING COMMUNITY

From its start, the Montgomery County Agricultural Fair drew not only farmers but also visitors from around the region who could enjoy the excitement of horse racing, see exotic and exciting performances and admire the handiwork of local farm families.

Each year, the fair organizers issued a program that listed the rules, the categories for competition and the premiums to be awarded and the schedule of events. A "greeting" in the 1914 program boasted of local skills and sociability: "Every year the fine carriages of the country people are gathered under the trees and lifelong friendships are renewed and memories of bygone days are revived, while the display of good things to eat and the beautiful work of the fair hands of the ladies in the Exhibition Hall testify to the boundless hospitality of the homes and the culture and refinement of their makers, which have always been the crowning virtues of the ladies of the County."

The fair programs also included advertisements that reflect the county's changing character. The 1876 program includes ads for merchants in downtown Washington, many clustered around the Center Market at 7th Street and Pennsylvania Avenue, offering guano, hardware, agricultural implements, dry goods, furniture, clothing and groceries (including "unrivalled Harvest Queen Family and Silverspring Extra Flour"), along with teas, wines, brandies and "segars." They touted their fertilizers like Peruvian guano, E. Frank Coe's super phosphate of lime and "Moore's pure soft ground blue Windsor plaster."

By 1914, M. Randall on Wisconsin Avenue in the District was offering "Cleaning, Dyeing, Altering and Repairing of Ladies' and Gentlemen's Garments, free collection and delivery," work that once would have been done at home. But work was changing; Strayer's Business College at 9th and F Streets advertised "Civil Service Preparation." There were also more local businesses— Oscar L. Johnson Building Material in Rockville; Dr. B.P. Wilson, a dentist who administered gas; the Montgomery County National Bank; and C.A. Fulks and Bro. offering automobile supplies in Gaithersburg.

By 1918, it was clear that farming was mechanizing. Ads for Fulton Motor Trucks claimed that they were a "modern farming necessity" that would "help you get your produce to market." The

Lyndall Motor Truck Company offered a Dearborn Truck Unit that could convert "a FORD or ANY other car into a Dearborn One or Two-Ton Truck." But there was still a call for Harry Poss, who sold Columbia Carriages in Rockville, and blacksmithing by Joseph W. Howes in Rockville, although he also advertised oxy-acetylene welding. Milking machines were advertised just below the new Cabin John Park subdivision, "pleasant and attractive homes or profitable investments."

In the 1920s and '30s, there were more ads and competition categories for suburban residents. Ads included mortgage companies, the A&P and Sanitary Grocery and "domestic engineering" products—boilers, lighting, plumbing, ranges and stoves. Competitors could show house plants like fuchsia, coleus and geranium, as well as antique items fifty years or older and arts like china painting, photography and drawing.

In 1931, the Agricultural Society's minutes record the public's "increasing apathy" toward the fair, so it was reduced to three days instead of four, admission went from seventy-five cents to fifty cents and fees for concession booths were lowered by 60 percent. By 1935, the society had sold the fairgrounds to the Montgomery County School Board, and it is now the site of Richard Montgomery High School.

as well as sheep and poultry diseases. Surrounding farms provided animal feed, and some families used milk and cream from the farm. By the 1920s, complaints from new neighbors had begun, and by 1936, the land had been turned over to the Maryland–National Capital Park and Planning Commission for parkland.

Life was changing. Alexander "Boss" Shepherd guided a post–Civil War building boom, developing and modernizing the city with development that extended through the city's northwest neighborhoods and into Montgomery County. Private telephone companies began limited service in 1894 around Sandy Spring, the Chevy Chase Land Company started buying farms and some Bethesda/Chevy Chase area farmers were dividing their land into half-acre lots. Eventually, this shift in population and commercial concerns would also shift political power from up-county farms to down-county suburbs.

The way people got their food and how they preserved and prepared it was also changing. Thomas Moore's "refrigeratory" drifted out of patent because ice wasn't readily available, but as Eleanor M.V. Cook recounted for the *Montgomery County Story*, an ice-box refrigerator cost about fifteen dollars for a wooden chest, lined with galvanized steel with a compartment on top for a block of ice, delivered to the house. Corncobs that had once fueled the smoking in farmstead meat houses could now be used to fuel the "ranges" sold by Sears, which could also be fueled by coal or coke for customers without ready access to cornfields.

Tracing advertisements, Cook noted there were more shops, taking the production of food and medicine out of the home. It's easy to see how Elizabeth Ellicott Lea's recommendations for Onion Poultice, Liverwort Syrup or a Molasses Posset for a Cold would be replaced by the convenience of "Vinsons emulsion of cod liver oil with hypophosphites for cough, colds, consumption, debility, dyspepsia and nervous prostration." And why bother with a sturdy farm breakfast of flannel cakes, eggs and sausage when you could get Shredded Wheat biscuits or Grape-Nuts from D.H. Bouie in Rockville.

Miss Mary Brooke was awarded a premium in 1910 for her Maryland biscuits, but the agricultural fair premiums are modest rewards, more of a reimbursement for materials. The real prize is a ribbon. *Courtesy Montgomery History.*

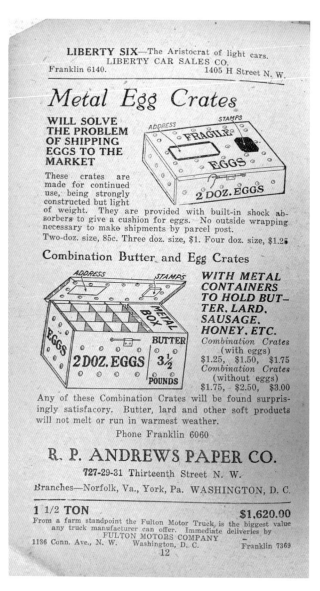

Technologies may change, but the issues don't. Getting a product to market safely and promptly, with as little waste and damage as possible, is vital to a successful farm operation. *Courtesy Montgomery History.*

And it could be delivered by automobile. Cook found that in 1900, the *Sentinel* reported, "'The automobile is being used quite extensively by many of the larger retail emporiums in large cities for the delivery of packages.' A Washington merchant had acquired an automobile adapted to this use, and 'this wonderful vehicle, which is now being used and admired throughout the county, will be on exhibition at the Agricultural Fair.'" This was a technology that would change the way land was used and valued.

The Chevy Chase Hunt is part of a Maryland tradition, although proponents point out that it should more accurately be called fox chasing; it seems more of an excuse to enjoy the countryside. But that countryside has shifted. In 1930, the Chevy Chase Hunt was displaced by development and merged with the Potomac Hunt. In 1980, the Potomac Hunt moved from Glen Road, farther out to Barnesville. *Courtesy Library of Congress.*

Water mains and sewers were installed on Diamond Road in Gaithersburg between 1926 and 1928 in a recognition of the services needed by the county's increasing suburban population. *Courtesy Montgomery History.*

Social life often included food. The annual Agricultural Fair was a social occasion, and the 1876 program for the twenty-third exhibition notes that "[t]he Society have fitted up a Boarding Saloon or Restaurant Building, in which visitors can be supplied with meals at hotel prices." The annual meeting of the Sandy Spring Farmers' Convention adjourned for a lunch prepared by the Ladies Committee—a very local meal prepared from the membership dues of "a basket food sufficient for six people." Food was also an excuse to socialize, like going chestnut hunting near Edward's Ferry.

Events around food were popular fundraisers, anticipated every year—strawberry and ice cream festivals in the spring and summer, oyster suppers or a cakewalk, where dancers competed for donated cakes. On May 5, 1899, a "grand old-fashioned cake walk" was held in the town hall in Rockville for the benefit of the newly organized Rockville Base Ball Club. Through the 1960s, the St. John's Episcopal Church in Bethesda held strawberry and apple festivals, as well as fundraising dinners, as a way to generate income and meet neighbors. You can still find an occasional cakewalk at elementary school fairs, although rather than dancing, winners try their luck in picking a number from a spinning wheel, and the Cabin John Strawberry Festival is still an annual event.

The Quaker communities around Sandy Spring gathered in many social clubs. The earliest farmers' club was founded in 1844 and later split into clubs of older and younger members. Most met monthly in a member's home who would also host a family-style meal. At one point, a member commented, "We meet to eat." In 1919, *The Annals of Sandy Spring* recorded a series of meetings in October—the Mutual Improvement Association on the fourth, the Home Interest Club on the sixth, the Horticultural Society on the seventh, the Wednesday Club on the eighth, the Neighbors Club on the ninth and the Enterprise and Montgomery Farmers Club on the eleventh. A visitor commented, "Sandy Spring can get up more occasions for fried chicken than any place I ever saw."

After the Civil War, communities around the country used cookbooks as fundraisers, often to support veterans' hospitals and memorials and often affiliated with churches. As women earned money by publishing their cooking and housekeeping expertise, the money they raised gave them a stronger voice in community affairs and institutions. Montgomery County had its own example, the *Up-to-Date Cookbook of Tested Recipes*, "compiled and published by Mrs. Spencer Watkins and Mrs. Francis F. Field." It seems to be based on a template; the Ladies Aid Society of the Mount Zion Church in Spring Grove, Pennsylvania, also compiled an *Up-to-Date*

The young women of Sandy Spring who enjoyed their leisure time at Camp Dismal had a sense of humor about their cooking. Their nine-page, ribbon-bound cookbook reveals some of the campers' misadventures: "Stuffed Eggs: (To be used when eggs for breakfast get too hard). Take off shells and cut eggs in two; take out yolks and mash with 2 tablespoons of butter and one of cream. Salt pepper and onion juice to taste. Refill whites and stick together (if possible). Roll in bread crumbs & egg, and fry in lard. N.B. If the eggs are not hard enough, they serve as a good top-dressing for a neighbors grass field." *Courtesy Sandy Spring Museum Archives.*

Cookbook, and many of the Montgomery County version's recipes also appear in a Kenton, Ohio edition.

Mrs. Spencer Watkins was born Maria Brooke and lived with her father and sisters at Oakland plantation, where they owned slaves. Her Southern loyalties were recorded by Horace H. Shaw in *The First Maine Heavy Artillery, 1861–1865*. Shaw described her as self-reliant and resourceful but "convinced that all this fuss and war, this loss and suffering, and this excitement, was due to the wild imaginings, perverse distractions, and evil intent of Northern Yankees." She was suspicious of Northerners and learned to shoot to defend her family's farm from the depredations of troops who would steal chickens or turkeys. But her attitude seems to have been turned by the Maine Regiment. Her family enjoyed the regimental band's music, she rode with the officers and their wives and she eventually dined with them. Shaw finished by writing, "She is a loyal Unionist now. She married Mr. Spencer Watkins…and writes of her love for the First Maine as one of the sweetest memories of her young life."

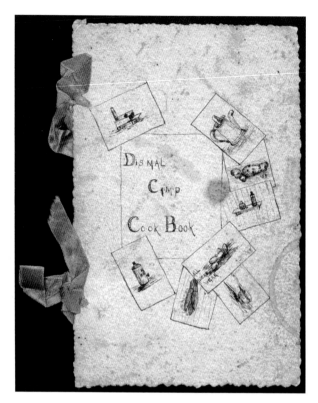

The nine-page, ribbon-bound *Camp Dismal Cookbook* makes camp life sound anything but dismal, and commentary on the recipes notes that the broken pieces of peppermint drops should be served first, that lemonade made with citric acid is "very poor at that" and that lemon candy should be boiled until it burns and "when cool—throw away." *Courtesy Sandy Spring Museum Archives.*

A project of her married years, the *Up-to-Date Cookbook* was compiled in 1897 to benefit St. John's Norwood Episcopal Church in Bethesda. The Watkinses were founding members in 1874, and the church was built on land donated by the Dodge family, neighbors of the Watkins's farm. The book's recipes feature dishes with a Maryland heritage—Delicious Turtle Soup, crabs in various preparations (but not crab cakes), terrapin, head cheese, hot slaw, Maryland biscuits and beat biscuits. It includes a homey recipe for potato pie made with lemon peel, sugar, wine and nutmeg on the same page as one for elegant cream puffs. There are also recipes with a Southern heritage, including okra soup, gumbo, South Carolina corn bread, Superior Rice Waffles and Owendaw cornbread (a kind of spoonbread). Mrs. Robert E. Lee's family cookbook includes a recipe for Owendaw cornbread made with hot cooked grits as well as cornmeal. (Mrs. Lee was a niece of Martha Custis Washington, whose granddaughter would live at Montevideo off River Road.)

The book's recipes also reflect a move toward Victorian-era elegance and the increasing availability of luxury grocery items—quite different from the sturdy farm cooking of Elizabeth Ellicott Lea. Dishes are deviled, escalloped and formed into croquettes. Salads are served on nests of lettuce, scooped into hollowed-out tomatoes, arranged and garnished. Creamed Turkey with Mushrooms is served in patty shells, and a recipe for Pate de Foie Gras sandwiches offers a substitution: caviar.

Further sophistication comes from "ethnic" recipes, including three uncredited Cuban dishes and a recipe for Macaroni a L'Italienne that asks for "12 sticks of macaroni" in a sauce of cream, butter, flour, cheese and milk, spiced with mustard and paprika. Mrs. M.C.D. Johnson, who shared this recipe, makes this suggestion: "If the sauce and macaroni stand long after being mixed the dish will be spoiled, therefore, if they cannot be served immediately, keep both hot on separate dishes. As it is awkward to serve the macaroni in unbroken sticks, some prefer to break the sticks before boiling, but the true Italian way is to serve with unbroken sticks."

The *Up-to-Date Cookbook* also includes advertisements for local merchants—all in the District and Georgetown, none in Baltimore or Montgomery County. Grocers, restaurants, a wood finishing mill, a jeweler, a hatter and furrier offer "dry and fancy goods," "candies carefully packed" and a "specialty furnishing house."

Unlike Ellicott Lea's very sensible *Domestic Cookery*, which was a tool to help manage a farm and its production, the *Up-to-Date Cookbook* can be seen as a reflection of the county's shift from farming to a more urban and suburban character—supporting a church in down-county Bethesda, advertising commercial establishments in D.C. and offering recipes that mix practicality with more elegant preparations meant to reflect wealth and sophistication.

But many county residents still measured their days and larders by the season. In an oral history for the *Potomac Adventure*, Anson Ball recalled, "In the fall, we'd store up for winter, like the squirrels.…[E]veryone had a barrel of flour and four or five sacks of corn meal, which had been ground at the local mill. [Mrs. Ball noted that the top of the flour barrel, turned upside down, was a bread board.] When it was time for hog butchering, neighbors got together and helped each other out. Women made lard, sausage and pannhaus scrapple. The ladies canned tomatoes, apple sauce and fruit. Peaches and apples were dried and corn cut off the cob and spread out to dry in the sun."

The women of Sandy Spring's Mutual Improvement Association kept meticulous minutes of their meetings, which, circa 1905, included reports from traveling members, exhortations to good works and good thoughts,

Cookbooks reflect our communities. Elizabeth Ellicott Lea was giving instruction on running a successful farm. A generation later, Mrs. Spencer Watkins was fundraising, while other cookbooks of the time were striving to make cookery a science. Measured ingredients and consistent cooking times removed intuition from cooking. But as this 1902 class at the National Seminary shows, cooking was part of women's work. *Courtesy Montgomery History.*

readings of poems, newspaper editorials and discussion of topics that ranged from the value of old stamps and the scandal of adulterated milk to teaching techniques and a brief history of matchsticks.

As each woman shared, the topics also included housekeeping, gardening and food production and preservation. After presenting two sonnets, Alice Tyson also spoke on "Agricultural Prosperity," recounting that a "judge had declared that the 'hen was not an animal' but the writer was inclined to characterize her as 'a gold mine' giving most wonderful statistics to prove her value to the world at large, and the U.S in particular."

Hallie J. Bentley shared "a list of the many uses of salt; it is an emetic, it cures bee-stings, it is a remedy for rheumatism and prevents night-sweats and hemorrhages, it cleans china & tin, preserves meat, and purifies sinks, is an excellent tooth wash and a lotion for the eyes. These are a few of the many ways in which it conduces to the help of man while most of our 'poor relations' the animals crave it."

Emma Bond, "by request, described her complete new chicken house, warmed and lighted in the most approved manner, her feathered friends are repaying her intelligent, and even affectionate, care in a most satisfactory manner."

There were also reports that reflect the changing styles and preferences for food and dining. Mary G. Colt told of a "wedding in California which was conducted according to the gospel of the 'Simple Life,' the word 'obey' was omitted from the service and the newly married couple walked to their new home. They expect to eat nuts, fruit and uncooked food exclusively. We were told of a 'Health Food' restaurant on G. St. near 11th in Washington."

There was also a mild disagreement about sausage, which the women clearly either made themselves or oversaw its making: "A few present used both sage and thyme in sausage, the latter, it was claimed, made the article keep longer, but one woman opined this was because it was not so palatable, and the consumer could not eat so heartily, in consequence."

Finally, "Elizabeth T. Stabler created quite a ripple by a dissertation against oysters, which were declared to be an unsavoury heathenish dish, and an unwholesome article of food. Very few, if any agreed with the writer in thinking that the time was nearly at hand when all sensible people would discard the bivalve from their bills of fare."

One thing the group did agree on was that "daily bread and daily duty are among the sweetest of all possessions."

Food is integral to how we celebrate and share, and outings with families and friends often included something good to eat—a shared picnic, a sweet slice of watermelon or a cooling drink of water. *Courtesy Montgomery County Historical Society.*

Between 1917 and 1924, Fred Van Hoesen was the county's first cooperative extension agent, charged with bringing new agricultural technologies and methods to fields and farms where they could be tested. He recorded the work done on Montgomery County farms in a series of glass plate images. *Courtesy Montgomery History.*

In 1920, 78 percent of county land was farms. But land in down-county was more valuable for development than for farming, and land along streetcar and rail lines in Wheaton and Kensington turned to suburban development. In *Days at Cabin John*, Edith Armstrong described a rural life on the cusp of suburban development. Her husband's commute to his downtown job required a mile-long walk to the trolley, especially burdensome when carrying the milk home for his children. Armstrong set a vegetable garden, her neighbors kept chickens and when they bought a car, it was quite a new thing. In 1904, when the Glen Echo Chautauqua ended, the community incorporated as a town. One of its first ordinances prohibited keeping pigs and hogs and outlawed wandering goats and cows. Other residents of the era recall picking wild fruits and nuts, and new householders in Glen Echo Heights were allowed to keep chickens, horses, cows or goats but not pigs. Armstrong's neighbor Mrs. Hebbs fussed about newcomers involving themselves in community governance and their willingness to pay higher taxes for lights on the roads and a new school.

Nevertheless, neighbors came together for a church fundraising supper. The churchyard was weeded, and tickets were handled at the basement door for a country supper with homemade pickles and jellies on each table, cut glass bowls of applesauce, potato salad and slaw, platters of ham and delivery of fried chicken and corn hot from the kitchen. And for "sweet'nin," there was lemon pie. Fancy work was for sale on the way out—crocheted doilies and scarves, aprons and sunbonnets, handmade lace and trimmed pillowcases.

The extension of streetcars into Chevy Chase and Glen Echo changed how land was used and valued. They connected communities built on former farmland to steady jobs with the federal government. Both lines initially attracted riders with amusement parks at their termini and quickly supported land development.

Montgomery County farms and mills were disappearing; they couldn't compete with large-scale Midwest beef and wheat production, although dairying became important, especially for farms within striking distance of a rail line, and those farms turned to table crops—vegetable, poultry and eggs, corn, potatoes and milk.

At one time, there were more than five hundred dairy farms in the county, with the supporting businesses to make them profitable—the rail lines and scheduled milk trains to bring milk to D.C. markets, breeding farms for replacement cows and creameries that processed milk into dairy products.

In a 1900 newspaper ad for the Chevy Chase Farm Dairy, proprietor George Wise described his operation: "Established 1881. I try to serve the very best quality of milk it is possible for a man to produce. My herd and dairy farm are open to inspection at all times."

Dairy farming underscores the complexity and science of farming; breeding and judging are central to creating strong stock and profitable farms. The King family worked as dairy farmers for five generations, and their farms in the center of the county, north of Rockville, boasted the largest registered Holstein herd. The farm was described as a "Montgomery Landmark," just twenty miles from the Capitol. From their livestock breeding, they sold breeding lines to buyers in Russia, Europe and Japan and

In this 1932 image, the kitchen at Brooke Manor in Ashton is a historical artefact. County kitchens were changing from country hearths to modern conveniences. *Courtesy Library of Congress, Prints and Photographs Division.*

won Premier Breeder and Premier Exhibitor honors at dairy expositions in the United States. This success was the result of careful record-keeping and a scientifically directed breeding program.

Eventually, the investment dairy farms required couldn't be supported by market prices. As with an earlier generation of wheat and cattle farms, dairies consolidated into larger, midwestern operations and local farms were too small to compete. Farms in Bethesda and Chevy Chase were once considered "the country." Joseph Hardy ran the Goldsborough Farm at the end of what is now Massachusetts Avenue and was invited to an annual dinner in 1915 hosted by the Washington Riding and Hunt Club "as a compliment to the farmers over whose lands the members of the club ride in their fox hunts." Guests ranged from Silver Spring to Chevy Chase, Bethesda, Little Falls, Takoma Park and Rockville.

The program for 1914's Sixty-First Agricultural Fair reflected the changing community. Ads in the 1876 program were primarily for agricultural products and merchants in Baltimore and Washington, D.C.

This 1947 Pepco kitchen at 8209 Ellingson Drive in Chevy Chase demonstrates the clean, modern appeal of an electric kitchen, an almost laboratory-like space. But as early as 1914, the Washington Gas Light company was advertising gas kitchens in the Agricultural Fair program. *Courtesy Library of Congress, Theodor Horydczak Collection, Prints and Photographs Division.*

As wheat farming and milling moved to larger farms in the Midwest, Montgomery County farmers turned to dairying, with a growing market in D.C., train connections to markets and wholesale buyers for their milk. Careful breeding made Montgomery County dairy herds world-renowned. *Courtesy Library of Congress.*

By 1914, there were advertisements for suburban development: "North Chevy Chase; Best Suburban Property North of the City; Improved Streets, Granolithic Sidewalks, Shade Trees, Water, Sewers, Electric Light; Street cars through the property For plats, price, etc.; William H. Walker; 729 fifteenth Street, N.W."

Brokers advertised alongside mortgage banks and title companies. There were many more local businesses, including one that offered "Cleaning, Dyeing, Altering and Repairing of Ladies' and Gentlemen's Garments, free collection and delivery," exemplifying the changes in running a household—home arts, the mending, darning, starching and washing described by Elizabeth Ellicott Lea replaced by services outside the home.

That 1914 program also contains an advertisement for a "commission house," a middleman producer that would step into the market to produce branded food at large quantities for chain groceries, where more suburbanites expected to buy their food. "We buy all the BUTTER FAT we can get, which we use only in the manufacture of butter. It is thoroughly pasteurized before churning, therefore, it need not be from tested herds or inspected premises, no shipping permits necessary, need not be absolutely sweet when it reaches us."

In the 1920s, Millard Eldridge Peake Sr. ran the Bethesda Farm Dairy on Arlington Road, and lawsuits recounted in the *Washington Post* illustrate the growing conflict between farming and suburban development. First, the dairy was sued by a father who claimed that a milk bottle had fallen from the delivery truck and injured his son. In 1928, a second case was brought by a bicyclist who claimed that he was hit by the delivery truck. In 1930, the dairy was sold to a larger operation, Chevy Chase Dairy, which was established in 1885 and would itself be bought out in 1931 by the National Dairy Corporation.

A bit farther out was Ayrlawn Farm, a model dairy farm established by John C. Letts in the 1930s. Letts was described as a "millionaire grocer" in

> Just as produce farmers choose vegetables that will thrive in a given microclimate and will appeal to customers, dairy farmers build a herd based on the characteristics of the cow and its milk. The herd at Woodbourne Creamery in Mount Airy is composed of Golden Guernseys, so named for the beta carotene in their milk.
>
> - Jersey: small, efficient at converting grass into a rich milk high in protein and butterfat that is good for ice cream and cheese.
> - Holstein: the biggest breed, delivering lower-butterfat milk at high production rates.
> - Guernsey: one of the most efficient breeds, a medium-sized, docile cow giving milk high in protein, cream, vitamin D, vitamin A and calcium.

In his 1918 scrapbook, County Extension Agent Fred VanHoesen noted that this "pulverizing roller is proving to be one of the most efficient tools on the market for fining and firming the seed bed." But this new machine is still horse-drawn. *Courtesy Montgomery History.*

the *Washington Star,* and his gleaming barns and prize livestock became a visitor attraction. But this farm, too, on land adjacent to what is now the National Institutes of Health, was overtaken by suburban development. Two buildings became part of the Ayrlawn subdivision, and the farm's pasteurization barn became the Ayrlawn Elementary School's library, bookshelves placed in front of the white tile walls.

The number of dairy farms in the county peaked in 1952 at 321, but after World War II job opportunities in the D.C. region expanded and it became harder to find farmhands. At the same time, beginning in the 1940s, Americans began drinking less and less milk. With demand decreasing and costs increasing, selling for development seemed to be the smart move.

Alden and Charlotte Waugh Potter's Farm, 34 acres along McArthur Boulevard, was farmed by their son Lloyd through the 1930s and 1940s but was eventually taken by the government for an I-495 interchange. Records show a series of public sales of dairy farms, herds and equipment throughout the county: Merhl Mayne in Gaithersburg in 1949, Ned Allnutt in Dawsonville in 1960, Frank Palmer and his daughter in Olney in 1955 advertised "Holstein Dispersal," and the T.N. Berlage Farm near Brookeville was sold by its then owner, Carper Fender, in 1958. The Crown Farm in Gaithersburg was the last to be sold. It was established in 1864 and expanded through 1937. The farm benefited from road and rail connections to the D.C. market, but when I-270 was built within view, dairying became less profitable. In the 1950s, its new neighbor was the Washingtonian Country Club, and when the farm was sold in 2006, it was surrounded by suburban development. The tools and machinery included in the sale listing had become antiques, including horse tack and cast iron boiling kettles used in butchering.

While agriculture was and still is a significant part of the county's economy, it was beginning to recede in political power, as a way of life and as a shaper of the landscape. More and more residents would live in suburban communities and work in Washington, D.C. Land would be valued more and more for its development potential rather than soil quality, and seasons wouldn't be marked by farm tasks.

Scientific and Stylish Dishes—Creamed Turkey with Mushrooms

The recipes in the 1897 Up-to-Date Cookbook *capture a point in time between food produced on the family farm and food from factories and groceries, between the rural life of the up-county and the social life of the suburbanizing down-county. The book includes recipes like Corn Pone, Virginia Ash Cakes and Head Cheese, which requires cleaning the meat "with the utmost care" from a pig's head, boiling the bones for their gelatin, spicing the mixture and molding it. The recipe is presented in a matter-of-fact way, but in today's modern kitchens, it is a near impossibility. A sensible Chopped Cabbage Pickle appears just a few pages after the more exotic Pineapple and Cocoanut Preserves. The instructions for Fowl Saute with Peas finish with the note that the same technique can be used for squirrel. And there are instructions to Fringe Celery for Garnishing.*

From its title, the book conveys an attitude quite different from Elizabeth Ellicott Lea's sensible and straightforward Domestic Cookery. *This book promises to put the home cook in the current fashion. And the fashion at the time was exemplified by the Boston Cooking School, which in 1897 was run* by Fannie Farmer and graduating classes of women who brought scientific measurement and nutrition to home kitchens. In the last quarter of the nineteenth century, wrote historian Laura Shapiro, American cooks were struck with "culinary idealism" reflected in cookbooks, cooking schools and even at Chautauqua assemblies, which included a "cookery department that offered lessons in Chafing Dish Cookery, Some Simple Puddings, and a Dainty Breakfast."

These "tested recipes" would ennoble household work with scientific principles. "Science and technology were gaining the aura of divinity," wrote Shapiro, and while their husbands commuted to orderly offices, wives ran orderly households. The recipes also have a social component. These cooks aren't working to ensure root cellars and pantries that can take a family through the winter; there are abundant groceries a trolley ride away or waiting to be delivered. Instead, they make elegant, appropriate and stylish dishes—nothing that appears "messy on the plate." Nonetheless, Mrs. Watkins's recipe is a time-honored way to use leftovers, re-creating them into a new dish with a bit of sauce and presentation.

Creamed Turkey with Mushrooms

One pint of any kind of cold fowl cut in pieces about the size of dice and creamed. Half can mushrooms or same Quantity of Fresh Mushrooms; One Tablespoon Flour Creamed with Tablespoonful Butter. Serve in Patty Shells.

Mrs. Watkins

Mrs. Watkins's recipe is a most general road map toward dinner but using patty shells and canned mushrooms put her in the vanguard of elegance and convenience. The version here offers a few more signposts.

1 rib celery, diced
2 tablespoons butter
2 cups fresh mushrooms, stems removed and cut into a medium dice
Salt and pepper
1 tablespoon flour
¾ cup chicken stock
1 cup cooked turkey (or chicken) cut into a medium dice
2 tablespoons heavy cream (optional)
2 patty shells
Chopped parsley to garnish

Sauté the chopped celery in 1 tablespoon of butter over medium heat until translucent. Add the chopped mushrooms, seasoning them with salt and pepper, until they are tender and just browned.

Add the remaining butter, sprinkle with flour and cook another minute. Add the chicken stock, increase the heat and stir until the sauce thickens. Stir in the diced chicken and cook until the chicken is warm. Add the cream for a lighter-colored, richer sauce.

Spoon the mixture into the two patty shells and sprinkle with chopped parsley.

Note: You can buy frozen patty shells or assemble your own from slightly defrosted puff pastry dough.

Chapter 7

FOOD FOR GOOD TIMES AND BAD

*A*fter the Civil War, the county focused energy and investment on rebuilding production and markets, and farmers adjusted their production. But two world wars and an economic depression would again make food an important factor in governing and fighting. As with every war, during World War I, the population of Washington, D.C., increased—from 350,000 in 1914 to 526,000 by 1918. The region had to feed more people and, with men called to the draft, needed to reallocate manpower, supply troops abroad and provide allies with food. The Depression would call on local farm women to mobilize their home skills in a commercial arena, and World War II would again bring increased demand and limited labor availability. In each case, the land and people were called on to respond. After World War II, a burst of suburban development would change the county's landscape and power balance and put the county at the cutting edge of contemporary food trends—fast foods, commissary foods, regularized recipes for standardized production and shipping.

"Food Will Win the War" was a campaign of the U.S. Food Administration, overseen by Herbert Hoover, to encourage food conservation. During the war, food was seen as a political tool to support Europe, and Maryland took the campaign seriously. Governor Emerson Harrington outlined a seven-point program:

- Farmers should cultivate the largest acreage possible.
- Farmers should consult and cooperate with Extension Service specialists to ensure better and larger crops.

Even though machines might make farming more efficient, it had to be the right machine. In 1918, Van Hoesen noted, "the two-bottom outfit [as opposed to the four-bottom] is the popular size. It is easily handled by one man and very efficient both as to amount and quality of work done." *Courtesy Montgomery History.*

- Those not employed in agriculture-related jobs should assist in obtaining labor, purchasing and transporting implements and supplies and generally aiding farmers.
- Farmers should chiefly produce staples, giving them preference over perishable products.
- Groups should be organized for growing, canning and preserving food.
- Vacant lot and backyard gardening should be encouraged.
- The people of Maryland should cooperate in the development of agricultural resources "to meet successfully the conditions which confront us."

Individual efforts included Mrs. John H. Gassaway of Rockville, who "invited local ladies to her kitchen to make jelly for the boys at Camp Meade; they produced 106 glasses from this collective effort." Hog fat normally thrown away was used to make nitroglycerine for bombs, and children

The Greatest Crime in Christendom

To buy—to cook—to eat more than you need; to waste a single morsel of food that can be used—is a crime.

Ten million have died bravely on the field of battle. They at least had a chance. They gave their all willingly and unselfishly.

Over twenty million have died of starvation—without even a chance to fight. To these death has come only as a relief from torture worse than death—*starvation.*

It is *our* job—yours and ours—to *save food* so that the millions of starving people in Europe may have SOMETHING to eat.

Eat Less Waste Nothing

Live Simply—avoid all food waste.

Don't Waste Food

United States Food Administration
ILLINOIS EDUCATIONAL DIVISION
CHICAGO

Above: Posters lining the walls encourage farm production and thrifty housekeeping with slogans like "Food is Ammunition, Don't Waste It." *Courtesy Montgomery History.*

Left: In war, food is a vital military resource. Well-fed troops fight more effectively, and allies, whose farm fields are turned to battlefields, can be supported with supplied food. Limiting food waste can also prevent inflation and rationing. Today, Americans waste nearly 40 million tons of food every year, most of which creates methane gas and takes up landfill space. A little wartime thrift would help meet the USDA's and EPA's shared goal to cut the nation's food waste by 50 percent by the year 2030. *Courtesy National Archives.*

collected pits and nuts used to make gas masks. "Each respirator required seven pounds of pits."

In 1917, the Women's Land Army of America was formed at the encouragement of the Woman's National Farm and Garden Association. By 1918, it had recruited fifteen thousand women across America to work farms left behind by men who had been drafted. The organization arranged central shelters where the women would sleep and eat, supervised their work assignments and emphasized that the work was a patriotic duty and of national importance. The WLAA's New York office sent a questionnaire to each volunteer seeking their opinions on health, governance, recreation and food: "Do you think a ten minute rest with sandwiches at ten o'clock in the morning is advisable? What criticisms or suggestions have you to offer in regard to food?"

In their uniform of brimmed hats, gloves, blue shirt and overalls, these new farm workers, called "farmerettes," were given agricultural training and charged with ploughing, cultivating, thinning, weeding, hoeing, potato planting, fruit picking, sorting and packing for market; mowing, with scythe and mowing machine; and hay raking and pitching, as well as dairy work.

The WLAA also convinced local farmers of the value of these new workers, although some were skeptical of women's ability to keep up with farmwork. But Hugh Findlay, an "expert from the Agricultural Department" who taught intensive farming, listed "Things Mr. Findlay has observed among the many things Women can do." The list revealed not only what women could do but also what was grown, how it got to market and the work necessary to keep a farm operational—"thinning onion, beets, corn, etc.; sorting fruit, packing in boxes, wrapping; and keeping records, payrolls, shipping."

In Montgomery County, the Rockville and Ednor units of the District of Columbia Division of the WLAA were overseen by Amy C. Ransome, who started with 16 volunteers, including her daughters. In Rockville, Dr. Willis Moore, who was a former chief of the Weather Bureau, volunteered his farm. Eventually, the D.C. Division oversaw 150 workers who, according to a 1919 *Farmerette* newsletter, undertook planting, thinning, cultivating, hoeing, dairying, teaming, sawing wood and handling hay and grain.

In a 1918 "Memorandum of Work done by the National Service School Graduates in the Women's Land Army of America," women assigned to the Broad Creek Unit were given commendations for their war work on the farms. Amy W. Brooks's "practical application of wise principles of conduct and discipline" made the camp a success. She also planted, thinned and

Mr. Hugh Findlay, Expert from Agricultural Department
Teaching Intensive Farming at the
National Service School.
. . . . . .

Things Mr. Findlay has observed among the many things

GARDENS: Women can do.

1. Hand and Wheel Cultivation
2. Light Horse Cultivation
3. Sowing seed by hand and drills.
4. Thinning onion, beets, carrots, corn, etc.
5. Weeding by hand
6. Harvesting crops
7. Bunching vegetables for market
8. Hand spraying for insects and disease
9. Keeping tools in good condition - sharpening hoes
10. Care hot-beds and cold-frames (filling and managing)
11. Managing the irrigation system
12. Transplanting

ORCHARDS AND SMALL FRUITS:

1. Thin fruit (apples, peaches, etc.
2. Picking apples, peaches and berries (one woman picked 60 bu. apples in one day without stepping on a ladder)
3. Sorting fruit
4. Packing in boxes, wrapping.
5. Labelling boxes
6. Keeping records, pay-rolls, shipping.
7. Driving team for spraying
8. Pruning raspberries, blackberries, etc.
9. Transplanting strawberries
10. Investigation of fruit shipments
11. Pruning
12. Budding and grafting

GENERAL FARM:

1. Tractor
2. Feeding stock
3. Clean cows and horses
4. Milking cows
5. Care of Milk, separating (Wareland Dairy Farm, Norfolk, Mass.)
6. Delivering milk
7. Harvesting and driving horses
8. Keeping harness in repair (sew and oil)
9. Wash wagons
10. Keep wagons in repair (Jacks can be used to lift wheels)
11. Drop potatoes (no lifting of bags)
12. Cut potatoes
13. Plant cabbages by hand or machine
(At Arlington Women preferred)

Women's work and roles are often redefined in wartime, when labor and support are in demand—from Civil War nurses, World War I farmerettes and World War II riveters. *Courtesy Montgomery History.*

Above: Uniforms and badges helped bond the WLAA as workers performing a vital national service. *Courtesy Montgomery History.*

Opposite: Women's work at home and on farms has always been a vital but sometimes unnoticed and uncounted. Wartime work opened new opportunities for some women, but those opportunities didn't always last after the war. *Courtesy Montgomery History.*

cultivated strawberries. It was particularly noted that "one especially fine result of her willingness and ability to drive the motor truck full of crated strawberries weekly to the city market twelve and one-half miles away to release the farmer's son to do heavy plowing." Amy received a service stripe for her work. Susan Ransome, one of Amy Ransome's daughters, was tasked to various farms in the Rockville area, and that summer and fall she "shocked wheat, rye and oats," did other general farmwork, gathered small fruits, pitched hay and threshed grain.

The work seemed to be a distinct and memorable time in many of the women's lives. A 1918 newspaper advertisement invited former members to reunite and form a club. Susan Reading had been recruited to pick apples, and writing later to Amy Ransome from her home in Milwaukee, she

seemed to miss the sense of purpose, imagining that there were many more opportunities for "woman's work" in Washington: "Now that the war is over and we are settled down to normal life, I am often at a loss for something to occupy my time."

Montgomery County's proximity to the national capital has always supported its strong economy. Surges of population and economic activity come with war and changing administrations. New programs and policies are often tested in nearby communities—a source of money and ideas for changes that may extend throughout the country. After World War I, an increased population, drawn by steady jobs provided by an expanded federal government, created a new demand for housing and streetcar-connected suburbs made down-county land more profitable for development than farming.

In an oral history, Edward L. Stock Jr. recalled growing up in Bethesda in the 1910s and '20s. In 1916, when his family moved from the District to a farm between Bradley Boulevard and Offutt Road, it was a move "out to the country," even though there was a farm that ran from their D.C. home on Lanier Place down to the zoo. At their new home, the family kept cows, pigs and chicken for meat and eggs. They had farmhands, but Edward "helped." He recalled harvesting corn, gathering the stalks into shocks and then husking and grinding in the winter. Their neighbors were other small farms—the Offutts on Offutt Road and farms between Old Georgetown Road and in the Battery Park area.

Contracts, even handwritten ones, between farmers and landowners outline the details of operation and responsibility: who will supply water, fencing, fertilizers and so on and specify how payment will be made—in kind or in cash. *Courtesy Sandy Spring Museum Archives.*

There was an icehouse on Wisconsin Avenue and a grocery store on Elm Street where you could call in your order in the morning, and it would be delivered by horse and cart in the afternoon. About once a week, Stock recalled, his mother would be driven downtown to shop at the Center Market, on Constitution Avenue, taking along her sons to help and giving them lunch afterward at the Occidental in the Willard Hotel. It was more of an estate life than a farm life.

Even as farmland was beginning to disappear, farming continued, particularly in the up-county. As with landowners and farmers today, agreements were negotiated for use of the land. In 1911, Dr. S.I. Scott entered into an agreement with James W. Howes to farm his land, a farm called Rangely, in exchange for half the crops grown. Scott would

HONEY. According to T.H.S. Boyd, writing in 1879, "The keeping and propagation of Bees in the County is assuming considerable importance. It requires but small capital and a very limited amount of muscular labor, while attended with little or no risk." He went on to say, "Bee-keeping has become a science, and those who patiently learn their ways, have no fear of being stung....To such perfection has the art of raising honey been brought that, not a bee is sacrificed in taking away the honey, while the comb is even saved."

supply seed and fertilizer, and Howes would haul it at no charge. Howes would also have use of a house, a barn, a garden and "one-half of the fruit on farm." They worked out agreements on fencing, livestock and pasturage, and Howes agreed to haul grain to the mill and market at no charge. They would agree to what was planted and that "all work to be done in a farmer-like manner." It's a two-page contract that succinctly outlined the details of farming—land, operations, markets and investments of time, money and labor.

In *Mama Wears Two Aprons*, Margaret Coleman reported the findings of Wardney C. Snarr, the county's extension service agent in 1922, about farming in the county: "[H]e counted 2,145 farmers in the County, 35 apple orchards, and 23 peach orchards. And 10 acres of rutubagas." Coleman also recorded the increasing prosperity at the Davis and King farms. Both farms served the Washington, D.C. market, loading milk onto the train at the Germantown station. Macie King was able to hire help, and the Davises enjoyed piped-in hot water and a bathroom.

But the Depression swept away economic gains. When Edward Stock finished studying agriculture at Cornell in 1929, many of his friends went to Wall Street without much luck, but he wanted to be a farmer, an interest he developed after growing up on his family's farm. "Well, farming, the bottom dropped out of that too." He found a job with the Department of Agriculture's Federal-State Shipping Point Inspection Service, inspecting fruits and vegetables at shipping points, from cotton in Alabama to potatoes on Maryland's Eastern Shore.

The Depression was aggravated by a three-month drought in 1930. As reported by the *Sun*, it "burned up the corn in the meadows," and orchard fruit dropped from the trees. "Vegetable gardens have failed so dismally that farmers are buying food from the green grocers." The story goes on to say, "These are usually prosperous counties, [Frederick and Montgomery] populated by farmers with resources and ingenuity generally regarded above the average." At his farm, along Rockville Pike, Albert Fields made use of his ingenuity and resources to install a water pump with a new gasoline engine and used stockpiled corn for feeding since the pastures were gone. The drought cut his milk production by a quarter, but he gained no corresponding price increase.

While many farmers could grow food to feed their families, they still needed a cash crop to pay mortgages and taxes, as well as to buy shoes, medicine and college tuition. And they needed to find customers.

Blanche Corwin was the county's assistant extension agent; her work was managed through the Extension Service established at the University of Maryland by the 1914 Smith-Lever Act. The act established agricultural research stations at the nation's land grant colleges to bring improvements in farming, home economics and public policy to rural communities. It was a kind of R&D program for food production, recognizing the importance of farms and their produce to the national economy. In Montgomery County, Corwin traveled among farms as a home demonstration agent, sharing information on running a farm home.

She organized a Homemakers Club, which became a starting point for establishing the Montgomery County Farm Women's Cooperative Market in Bethesda, a response to the 70 percent drop in farm income. Farms were failing, and Corwin thought that a cooperative market in Bethesda, near federal workers and their steady paychecks, would be a way to generate income without a middleman.

On opening day in February 1932, in a rented space near the Edgemoor community, the nineteen women opened at 7:00 a.m. and nearly sold out of their cakes, bread, poultry, sausages and preserves. Alden and Charlotte Potter had bought their thirty-five-acre farm near the C&O Canal in 1920, and Charlotte was "one of the first to rent a stall the Montgomery County Farmwomen's Market where she sold produce from her garden, tarts and cookies from her kitchen, and firewood from her woodland."

Bill Duvall's grandmother, Macie King, was a founding member of the Market, and Duvall recalled that there was fierce opposition by businessmen and the community to the women having a business. Regardless, the women put up a tent and sold everything they had made and brought, including sausage, cured hams, potatoes, baked goods, sweet corn and sauerkraut. On Macie's farm, the children and tenant wives helped with the cooking, baking

Part of food's value comes from its provenance and presentation. Farm women in spotless aprons displaying products from their farms and kitchens had a different appeal than grocery stores, which were becoming more prevalent. *Courtesy Montgomery History.*

about fifty cakes a week. With her earnings, Macie installed an electric range in the basement, in addition to using a wood stove and range in the kitchen. Dressed chickens were a popular item, and one person was assigned to pluck the chickens. The Cissel Farm planted a succession of about six acres of sweet corn, every five days planting another six rows so that ripe corn came in through September. Lots of vegetables, like squash and beans, were planted just for the market. Duvall also recalled that a dairy farming family in Damascus who couldn't pay their taxes were invited to sell at the market. At first, they didn't think they had anything of interest, but when asked if they had firewood, cow manure or eggs, they found customers, even for the manure, used to fertilize down-county vegetable gardens and rose bushes.

By June, thirty-one women were selling, and the market moved to the corner of Wisconsin Avenue and Leland Street. By November, there were forty-two participants and a waiting list. Households reorganized themselves around the market, with children pitching in, leaving mothers time to bake or dress chickens for the Saturday market. Customers clamored for fresh, high-quality farm products—spareribs, hams and head cheese; milk, butter and cream; and relish, piccalilli and potato salad.

The market was a success, but when the women eyed the vacant Piggly Wiggly store near Edgemoor, it was too much for the posh neighborhood, whose residents enlisted political leader E. Brooke Lee to stamp out the idea. Corwin was fired, but the market continued under its tent. It was featured in *Reader's Digest* and would eventually count President Eisenhower, who placed a special order for Macie King's hominy grits, among its customers. The women wore white dresses and clean aprons, expanded the market hours to include Wednesday and priced their goods cooperatively.

Margaret Davis baked forty loaves of bread and twenty-five dozen rolls for each market day. Pearl King made ninety cakes. Macie King made beans and sauerkraut along with her cakes. Elsie Daniel sold dressed chickens, eggs, mint, zinnias, larkspur and her specialty: molded jellied chicken.

At a time when women were referred to by their husbands' names, couldn't serve on a jury and couldn't record their name on property deeds, the cooperative decided to buy a property on Wisconsin Avenue. By 1945, they were able to burn their mortgage after paying it off with the profits from jams, biscuits and sauerkraut.

At the Farm Women's Market, women used their domestic skills in a commercial arena to help support their families. Local and seasonal food has

After an initial outing under a tent, the Farm Women's Market was eventually able to secure a loan and build a permanent market building. The loan officer was convinced of their success when he saw the Saturday crowd of customers. *Courtesy Montgomery History.*

a market advantage, and value-added farm products like honey, soap, bread and cut flowers are traditional domestic products that can earn a premium for farmers. Even as local sellers have dwindled, the market endures and is a listed local historic site. It has diversified by providing weekday parking for neighboring office workers and a front yard flea market. The vendors have changed, and men may sell as well as women, but each stall is still an independent business.

The Farm Women's Market was eventually viewed as a unique and valuable local asset—part of a movement to support farm operations and sales. A *Bethesda Journal* article in 1940 described Juliane Waters's production for the market: 400 turkeys, 2,000 chickens and 110 hogs per year, with 2 hogs per week for every Saturday market. The reporter commented, "One need not stretch the imagination to realize what a profitable thing a farm could be with a fine market only a few miles away." A 1940 issue of the *Reader's Digest* reported, "The modernizing movement has proved to be contagious. 'The example of the women in the cooperative,' the agent told me, 'has put the county 50 years ahead in its agricultural ideas. It is no longer necessary to argue up-to-date farm practices. Even more important, we are proving to the youth of the county that farming can be made to pay and farm life can be made attractive.'"

It was a modernizing movement that wouldn't quite stick. Food would be important again during World War II, but after the war, the demand for housing, expanded federal jobs and increasing automation would make farm work seem less relevant in Montgomery County.

But in 1940, 68 percent of county land was in agricultural use, and farmers would again be called on to produce to meet war needs. In 1942, the Farmers' Convention of Montgomery County heard a speaker on the topic "Agriculture and Agricultural Adjustment in the War Effort." The speaker emphasized "the certainty of war or the necessity to win it." As in previous wars, the federal government involved itself in food production, setting goals to increase tomatoes and canning crops as well as dairy and poultry. As ever with bureaucracies, though, it seems unfamiliarity with the realities of farming and a plethora of uncoordinated programs bedeviled farmers.

Consumers were encouraged to do their part and were exhorted not to waste food. Food rationing began in 1942 with sugar and coffee. The federal government halted the sale of canned vegetables and froze the price of fresh vegetables. Rationing eventually extended to meat and those who could dealt directly with farmers. The rationing point system and

Bill Duvall remembered the three-part rolls that his grandmother Macie King made for Thanksgiving and Christmas, cooked in muffin tins. "When you took them apart the inside was like white cotton— so soft and white, like cotton. I just thought they were great." But somehow, when his mother made them they weren't the same; when he "carefully" asked why, his mother said, "Well, you know Billy, all Grandma used to use was pure lard." *Courtesy Montgomery History.*

shortages made people "food conscious," and home-based efforts at food production returned.

Between 1941 and 1942, Edward Stock was chairman of the local Victory Garden program, and he recalled it as one of the best experiences of his life because they "had all the resources of the University of Maryland in Beltsville…they really educated us." Many property owners donated land to the effort, and between the agricultural experiment station off Wisconsin Avenue just south of Chevy Chase Drive and another 150 gardens in Silver Spring on the site of what is now Holy Cross Hospital, the program was a success and evolved into the Men's Garden Club. They met at Bethesda Elementary School to get information for their backyard gardens and found that the county agent knew about livestock but not about vegetables and home gardens.

Farm work was often community work. In Sugarland, after the fields were harvested for market, neighbors would glean the fields and preserve what was harvested. Here, in 1937 Brookville, threshing took many hands. *Courtesy Library of Congress, photograph by Edwin Locke.*

The work wasn't only in the fields. Lunch had to be prepared and ready for hungry farmhands. *Courtesy Library of Congress, photograph by Edwin Locke.*

In his weekly columns for the *Bethesda Journal,* Stock encouraged beginning gardeners and advised them to start by lightening the local clay soil with sand and loam, choosing plants with "high food value" and allowing room for a row of zinnias, marigolds or calendula. "With a gay dining room table you may forget there isn't any steak to eat."

While the draft and increased wartime production eliminated unemployment, they also created a shortage of workers. In 1943, the *Washington Daily News* reported "Bethesda Boys Sign Up With Victory Corps." A crew of forty boys, aged twelve to sixteen, were paid twenty-five cents an hour to do odd jobs, like painting, carpentry, washing cars and mowing lawns. The article included a picture of Victory Garden Corps hoeing at the instruction of Edward Stock. According to Mrs. Chase Donaldson, the Bethesda Victory Gardens Committee chairman, it was "a patriotic corps to help the community." Some farmers made extra money by plowing and tilling these new gardens.

Likewise, there was a pressing need for skilled farm labor. The proceedings of the Farmers' Convention of Montgomery County noted that "vital" farmworkers could defer military service, and through the war, who and what was vital would be in constant negotiation. Many workers

Although not always the most reliable workers, schoolboys were encouraged to work on local farms. Here, "Carroll Dawn is too young to be in the Army, but he's just as important on this tractor as he'd be in a tank, for as Secretary of Agriculture Vickard says, 'Food will win the war and write the peace.'" *Courtesy Library of Congress, photograph by Howard Liberman.*

not drafted went to industry, CCC workers were reassigned to farm work and there was discussion of recruiting new farmerettes and using convict labor. Schoolboys were recruited to farm work. *A Pictorial History* recorded, "In June 1942, the United States Employment Service in Silver Spring registered 125 high school students to work on Montgomery County farms for the summer. Their wages were 25 cents per hour and they tied their lunches in the trees to protect them from dogs and ants," although later proceedings noted that of 160 boys recruited, only 69 showed up for work.

Other farms used German prisoners of war as farm labor. They lived in a camp near Emory Grove and were taken to farms each day, with a packed lunch of an apple and a sandwich; farmers weren't allowed to feed them for fear of poisoning. There was some suspicion on both sides. Jane and Emily Allnutt weren't allowed outside when the POWs were working on the farm. On the Allnutt farm they helped with threshing—on other farms they picked pumpkins.

According to Bill Duvall, a founding member of the Mooseum, there were about 450,000 Italian, Japanese and German POWs in camps nationwide. He recalled that in Montgomery County, there were about 200 low-ranking prisoners, with only a few officers. Farmers could pick up men in the morning and bring them back in the evening, paying the Agriculture Department a rate of 42.5 cents per hour per man. Bill related that his father signed them out by including their name, rank, date and what they'd be doing. Wesley Hargett had two or three POWs on their farm, and they became friendly. His son went to Germany in 1984 to meet the family.

There was demand for food as well as resources. The Convention notes state that the "average soldier consumes 2 pounds more per day than he did in civilian life," and farmers received incentive payments for vegetable crops of sweet potatoes, cabbage, carrots, lima beans and tomatoes. The State Committee for Farm Labor noted that in World War I it took five

Just as some women found work opportunities in factories and offices, others were called on to step outside their usual work roles. Here, in April 1942, "Mrs. Allie Messer of Montgomery County, MD, will do a man's part in getting her husband's land in shape for planting food for Victory crops." *Courtesy National Archives.*

agricultural and industrial workers to support one soldier, but by World War II, it took sixteen workers to support a soldier. Farmers were encouraged to use all their farm machinery, and what couldn't be used should be stripped for parts and scrap metal.

Just as Elizabeth Blair Lee's father received a good price for his wheat, sold to the government during the Civil War, wheat farmers during World War II also saw a price increase. In March 1941, the *Washington Post* reported that wheat prices "skyrocketed" by almost three cents per bushel and that commodities sales were strengthened by "prospects of passage of the lend lease bill and by the war situation."

After the war, the Convention proceedings reflect the changes in farming, in the county and in the region. They describe the transition from a "horse economy" to machines; the appearance of DDT, "a new chemical that has a definite place in farm operations"; and how a stroll along the Patuxent River prompted a discussion of WSSC's accelerated expansion from ninety-six miles square miles to serve 32,000 people to two hundred square miles, serving 200,000 people.

The meeting discussions revolve around balancing cost and profit, the search for farm labor, soil improvement and ways to make farming more efficient, including plant hybrids, livestock breeding and machines. Another regular topic is the frustration with government involvement in farming, from state plans to take land along proposed roadways to farm production policies. A.D. Farquhar's three-stanza poem recorded this frustration in rhyme and with humor:

> *You can get us sacked potatoes for a measly little cent*
> *Although these spuds cost dollars to the government,*
> *And the sack itself is equal to at least a quarter's worth*
> *Even thou it may be soiled with a bit of Mother Earth.*

He went on to lament the challenges of storing, shipping and pricing perishable crops like potatoes and seems to say that what the government won't meddle with, mother nature will:

> *Just leave us be if now and then a surplus should begin,*
> *Colorado beetle'll get our vines, mosaic gets our skin!*

In 1952, the Convention heard from Luther Bonham of the University of Maryland's Department of Agricultural Economy on "Planning for

While some farmers sold to wholesalers or commission houses that would transform produce into groceries, others still worked on local market schedules. *Courtesy Library of Congress, photograph by Marjory Collins.*

Prospective Suburban Development in Rural Areas," a title that makes it seem a given that farms would be turned over into residential neighborhoods. The proceedings describe "really comprehensive planning" as a "vague" and "painful idea," with a loss of freedom comparable to a totalitarian state.

Down-county farming was first to be overtaken by suburban development. Edward Stock had begun a lawn mowing business and then expanded into landscaping and a garden center. It was a business that thrived along with suburban development when land was used for appearance and display rather than production. After World War II, Arlington Road was extended, turning farms into house lots, and he recalled, "We had too many people coming around, wanting to buy the place." So, they moved, family and business, farther out to "the country"—twenty-two acres on Montrose Road—to land that had been a horse farm. They lived in the old barn that had been renovated into a house.

Bill Duvall pointed out that soldiers returned to the county from World War II with new skills and trades—they had employment options beyond the grueling work of farming seven days a week, from dawn through dusk. Steady work offered by the federal government or providing goods and services to the county's increasing suburban population was more appealing than the expense and risks of farming. As a result, farmers could no longer easily get farm labor paying low wages and offering tenant housing, which in turn made it harder to maintain a successful farm.

As suburbs expanded, the price of agricultural land jumped to more than $1,000 per acre. When a farmer died or retired, the next generation couldn't afford to keep the land and continue farming. By the 1960s, the price of land couldn't be supported by the earnings of a dairy farm. As Bill Duvall noted, "If you had a farm, you might be able to keep going, but to buy a farm, the price of milk wouldn't support it." In the 1980s, a federal government buy-out program supplemented dairy farm income with regional price differentials and by purchasing milk, cheese and butter. In 1983, the Dairy and Tobacco Adjustment Act bought out farmers' herds with the goal of ending an oversupply of milk and adjusting the market. It was the moment for change.

The growth of the federal government after two world wars had a dramatic effect on surrounding Maryland and Virginia counties. Rural and agricultural in the nineteenth century, they shifted to become suburbs of Washington, D.C., providing housing and communities for federal workers. To direct and accommodate this change in lifestyle, economy and land use, a number of regional planning and public service agencies were established. In D.C., the National Capital Planning Commission was established in 1926 to address city and regional planning—including land use, streets, parks, parkways and recreation, mass transportation and community facilities—and to coordinate the plans of federal district departments.

This comprehensive approach was expanded into Montgomery and Prince George's Counties with the establishment of the Maryland-National Capital Park and Planning Commission (M-NCPPC) in 1927. The two commissions planned for the expansion of infrastructure, water and sewer, roads and parkland within a defined Regional District, which included

Transportation, an expanded market and new employment opportunities changed the way people ate. Food came from the market, not the farm. In 1941, the *Washington Post* reported on a new phenomenon: the supermarket. It described "glittering immensity," a "perambulator parade" of shopping carts and the temptation of bulk bargains that any contemporary warehouse shopper would recognize. *Courtesy Library of Congress, photograph by Howard Liberman.*

only some of the land in each of both counties. In Montgomery County, it included the suburbanizing down-county, not the rural up-county areas. The county's first zoning plan in 1928 separated residential from commercial and industrial uses and set standards for residential lots.

The M-NCPPC 1954 Annual Report records the change in farmland, with photos of county crossroads like Georgia Avenue in Wheaton transformed from fields and a few stores to an unrecognizable pattern of new roads, houses, playgrounds, shopping centers and recreation centers. Bar charts record the explosion in lots recorded; maps track increases in population, illustrate land-use studies and survey zoning and road expansions, including an "Outer-belt Freeway" designed to serve "outlying areas," crossing Connecticut and Georgia Avenues in Silver Spring. "Outlying" was shifting farther and farther out.

Both the Convention and planners recognized that the spread of suburban development was changing how the county looked, worked and lived and would bring a "consequent disorganization of the economic life" in rural areas. But the bulleted planning goals were meant to be reassuring, including "protecting the base of agriculture, with the tax rate not affected."

The next planning steps that would redefine the county's land use were the 1955 Master Plan of Highways and the 1957 General Plan. That plan defined a pattern of "wedges and corridors" that roughly kept development within defined areas. Nonetheless, once the entire county was included in the Regional District and comprehensively zoned, agricultural land would be judged not only for its fertility but also for its development potential. Comprehensive planning would eventually lead to the creation of the Agricultural Reserve through rezoning and easements (with a lower tax rate as a result) that would protect a significant amount of the county's farmland.

As down-county farms became suburban neighborhoods, they filled in with suburban services like supermarkets, geared toward families and cars. By the 1930s, Bethesda had three Sanitary Stores supermarkets. It was a change that had begun in the 1920s and that caught the canny eye of J. Willard "Bill" Marriott.

Returning home to Utah from his Mormon mission in New England, Bill Marriott stopped in D.C. on a hot August day in 1919, and this gave him the idea to open an A&W root beer stand. He researched the franchise, bought in with a friend and returned to D.C. with his wife, Alice, in 1927 to open his first stand.

His first location was in a small storefront at 14th and Kenyon Streets, NW, one of D.C.'s busy five-way intersections in what is now the Columbia Heights neighborhood. He expanded to other locations, all chosen with attention to the number of cars passing by and their direction. The third stand, on Georgia Avenue, was a drive-in, a new type of restaurant that required a curb cut driveway entrance, which was only allowed for gas stations. Marriott persisted, got his curb cut and put himself ahead of the trend for increased car ownership that would change the landscape.

Another innovation were the curbside servers, dubbed "running boys," who brought food to customers waiting in their cars. But even though Bill Marriott was innovating the way his customers ate, he treated his business in the hands-on way a farmer knows his fields. His sharp eye for change and attention to customers are reminiscent of the ingenuity and market innovations displayed by the county's Quaker farm community. He was, his son recalled, "a great believer in the principle of 'management by walking around,'" inspecting, noticing and correcting.

At Hot Shoppes and other "fast food" outlets, food was sustenance, but it was also served with an element of novelty and entertainment. Bill Marriott would expand his local chain of family restaurants into a worldwide hospitality business serving institutions, airlines and individual travelers. *Courtesy Library of Congress, photograph by Marjory Collins.*

Just as farms felt the Depression, so did the Hot Shoppes. Marriott managed to keep his employees, but customers had to be found in new locations with new enticements. To lure customers, Hot Shoppes offered promotion tickets with the slogan "Food for the Family," aiming beyond the initial market of office workers to reach them at home and develop a steady customer base. They also expanded to follow customers into the suburbs, first at 4340 Connecticut Avenue, on the Montgomery County border, and then out Connecticut Avenue into other Montgomery County locations in Silver Spring Friendship Heights. By 1941, Hot Shoppes had opened at the corner of Wisconsin Avenue and East-West Highway in Bethesda, a location that became a favorite with Bethesda–Chevy Chase High School students.

In fact, Bill Marriott was at the forefront of creating the industrialized food system that we take for granted today. As the business expanded, he standardized recipes and operations in accounting, administration and customer relations. Food production was centralized in a Silver Spring commissary and delivered out of a River Road warehouse. The restaurants' design created a recognizable brand, and the Hot Shoppes became a regular part of community life—an after-school meeting place, a bite after shopping, an office lunch and a tourist oasis.

But more than just a chain of coffee shops, Marriott put his business at the forefront of an expanding regional, national and eventually global network of food production. The company expanded to serve government cafeterias and offer airline catering services. By comparison, the Farm Women's Market operated at the other end of the spectrum, taking value from small-scale, local products that one cook could prepare in her kitchen.

In 1950, 67 percent of the county was in farmland, but between 1954 and 1964, that land increased in value by 330 percent, from $301 per acre to $1,302 per acre. Montgomery land was worth twice that in Frederick or Carroll Counties. Farmers could sell to developers and then buy a farm in Frederick and still have cash to upgrade operations. Dairy moved to Loudoun or farther, some farmers retired, some downsized and some developed. It became expensive to own land and hard to find farm labor.

Not everyone was ready to give up farming. In 1965, Esther Scott entered into an agreement with Milton Turner to rent Plainfield Farm, with terms specifically spelled out. Scott and Turner agreed on the rent, but Scott also clarified improvements like fencing and a tenant house, removing and reusing rocks from one of the fields and fields used for hay, corn and her small cattle herd.

Later that year, she requested and received a special exception for a "wayside stand" on Layhill Road, one-half mile south of Sandy Spring, where she would sell vegetables from her garden, with the help of her farm tenant, Mrs. Stone. From another special exception, Scott also ran a sawmill at this site. The petition commented, "There has been no change in the neighborhood. The sawmill cannot be seen from the road. There have been no complaints—only approval from the neighbors."

MONTGOMERY COUNTY FARMLAND
1950: 213,004 acres
1954: 197,335 acres
1964: 155,300 acres
1974: 102,000 acres (very close to the 93,000 acres
of the Agricultural Reserve)

Form 3 (Revised 10-3-62)

Docket No. _____

Date Filed _____

COUNTY BOARD OF APPEALS
FOR
MONTGOMERY COUNTY

Date Hearing _____

Decision: Granted _____

Denied _____

Other action _____

PETITION FOR SPECIAL EXCEPTION UNDER ZONING ORDINANCE
PLEASE NOTE INSTRUCTIONS ON REVERSE SIDE.
ATTACH AND REFER TO ADDITIONAL SHEETS IF SPACES
FOR ANSWERS ARE TOO SHORT.

Petition is hereby made for a special exception under the Zoning Ordinance for the Maryland-Washington Regional District in Montgomery County, Maryland, (Chap. 104, Mont. Co. Code 1960, as amended) as follows:
Approx. 5 acres
Property to be used: Lot _____. Block _____. Subdivision _____
one mile South of
Town Sandy Spring. Street and No. Route 182 . Zone Classification RA .
Use proposed _____

Zoning Ordinance subsection providing for proposed use: Sec. 104-29 104-29 .
Owner of property: Name Esther W. Scott
Address Sandy Spring, Maryland
Petitioner's present legal interest in above property: (check one)
☑ Owner (including joint ownership) ☐ Lessee ☐ Tenant other than as lessee (describe) _____

☐ Contract to lease or rent. ☐ Contract to purchase. ☐ Other (describe) _____

Has any previous petition or appeal involving this property been made to this Board, or to the former Board of Zoning Appeals, by this Petitioner, or by anyone else to this Petitioner's knowledge? Yes . If so, give Case Number(s): 1285

Further comments, if any: There has been no change in the neighborhood. The sawmill can not be seen from the road. There have been no complaints - only approval from neighbors.
I have read the instructions on the reverse side of this form, and am filing herewith all of the required accompanying information.

I hereby affirm that all of the statements and information contained in or filed with this petition are true and correct.

Esther W Scott
SIGNATURE OF PETITIONER

Sandy Spring, Md.
ADDRESS OF PETITIONER

(OVER)

Wa. 4 3421
PHONE NUMBER

In 1965, Esther Scott worked out the details of a contract, special exception and permits to continue farming and operating a sawmill on Plainfield Farm off Layhill Road. Her special exception application for the mill noted, "[T]here has been no change in the neighborhood. The saw mill can not be seen from the road. There have been no complaints—only approval from the neighbors." *Courtesy Sandy Spring Museum Archives.*

Up-county businesses served locals and visitors looking for a day in the country. Intersections are often good for business. At Maryland Routes 28 and 109, the Darby Store was established around 1910, and across the street was Staub's Country Inn, established in 1944. The late nineteenth-century building housed both the restaurant and Beallsville's tiny post office. The restaurant had a jukebox, a counter and a few tables with gas pumps out front. Ginger Hoffacker, whose aunt and uncle ran it, recalled that "sweet tea was a big thing, as well as milkshakes made from hand dipped ice cream." Uncle Charles was also the postmaster, and the restaurant was a social place, with locals coming in for their morning coffee.

Montgomery County retained its agricultural economy and land even as suburbs spread and food production became global. T.H.S. Boyd's 1879 estimation of the impact of the recently opened Metropolitan Branch Railroad seems a fair summary of the challenge that faces the county and the Reserve today. While Boyd saw proximity to the national capital as an unalloyed good—not imagining that development would eclipse farming—he also saw the area's value for a range of uses:

> *As the location of Washington seems to be on ground prepared for a site of the seat of Government of a great Nation, so Montgomery County seems prepared to furnish supplies of all kinds for the inhabitants of such a city; Milk, Butter, Poultry, Hay, Fruit, and Vegetables, in fact, everything which will not stand long carriage. Also, by means of this road, to furnish locations for country residences for those who can afford it, the whole line from Washington to Sugar Loaf Mountain furnishes sites for cottages, where abundant water of best quality, shade trees and soil most favorable for gardeners can be found.*

This conflict between farming and development was forestalled by envisioning and establishing the Reserve through county master plans. The initial act was supported with policy decisions that buttressed the notion of limited development in the Reserve (removal of outer beltway, rustic roads, sewer and water limits), but now that vision must be supported by ongoing policy refinements that support active agricultural uses.

Policy challenges remain in creating the Reserve as a place, as Boyd wrote, "prepared to furnish supplies...which will not stand long carriage." We don't worry about "long carriage" today, as our food is distributed via a global food chain, but we are learning the value of local food. Not only does it taste better, but its seasonal nature ties us to nature's cycles and

STRAWBERRIES. *Fragaria virginiana* is a native plant that has been cultivated into many varieties for flavor, climate and shipping. Montgomery County farms grow this high-value crop, but among the best are those you pick yourself at local farms that have been growing for generations, including Butler's Orchard and Homestead Farm.

provides a kind of food security, while local production creates local jobs and preserves local land.

Aside from particular local issues, farming in Montgomery County faces the same challenges that farms across America are grappling with. In its "Farms Under Threat" study, the American Farmland Trust has mapped the conversion of agricultural land into development that weakens farm viability and found that between 2001 and 2016, the United States lost 11 million acres of agricultural land and that the largest threat comes from large-lot housing development.

Saving one-third of Montgomery County for agriculture and open space was a bold move in the face of the money to be made by meeting development demand in the national capital. It required meticulous technical work to overlay land characteristics and define the area of the Reserve. It called for attentive political maneuvering to balance the expectations of farmers, landowners and developers.

That balance is illustrated in Wade Butler's family's experience with their farm business. His parents had some success with various crops and products, finally settling on one of the first pick-your-own farms. They had such success that they decided to expand, but land prices forced them to consider sites as far away as Pennsylvania, which would require reconceiving the business and would create new costs and investments. But the rezoning that was part of creating the Agricultural Reserve made neighboring land more affordable. Butler recalled that their neighbor was initially unhappy with the rezoning, losing the anticipated increase he'd gain by selling to developers, but the neighbor sold his land to Butler's and became a valued informal partner in their operations.

Food for the Family—Mighty Mo and Orange Freeze

Longtime residents remember the Mighty Mo hamburger, which, in 1955, sold for fifty cents. Alongside an Orange Freeze, it was the quintessential Hot Shoppes meal. When the recipe was translated from the corporate instruction card to a cookbook meant for home kitchens, measurements changed from ounces to tablespoons. Likewise, the service instructions were deleted. Home cooks couldn't order the Mighty Mo sauce from the commissary and didn't have to serve the burger on a #3 plate or "Wrap the sandwich in special Mighty Mo paper—15" by 10¾"."

This version is adapted from Marriott Hot Shoppes Cookbook: Sixty Years of American Cookery, *published in 1987, thirty years after the last Hot Shoppes was built in 1967 and eight years before the Bethesda Hot Shoppes closed in 1995.*

Mighty Mo Sauce
½ cup ketchup
¼ cup chili sauce
1 ½ teaspoons A.1. Sauce
½ teaspoon Worcestershire sauce
2 drops Tabasco Sauce
½ cup finely chopped sweet pickle
1 ¼ cups mayonnaise

Blend the ingredients and set aside.

Mighty Mo Sandwich
1 sesame seed bun, cut crosswise into 3 slices
1 tablespoon margarine
2 ⅛-pound hamburger patties
Salt and pepper to taste
1 slice American cheese
4 teaspoons Mighty Mo sauce
1 tablespoon shredded lettuce
2 dill pickle chips

Spread the cut surfaces of the sliced bun with margarine and set aside. Season the hamburger patties with salt and pepper, and grill them, being careful not to overcook them. Top one with the slice of cheese.

A Culinary History of Montgomery County, Maryland

Spread some sauce on the bottom bun, top with shredded lettuce, the hamburger patty and the center slice. Spread that slice with sauce and the cheeseburger patty. Top with dill pickle chips and the bun and spread with the remaining sauce.

Orange Freeze
¾ cup fresh (or from frozen) orange juice
1 cup orange sherbet
Orange slices, maraschino cherries, fresh mint (to garnish)

Chill two tall glasses in the freezer. Blend the orange juice and sherbet in food processor or blender to the consistency of a milkshake—don't over blend or it will become thin. Pour into the chilled glasses, garnish and serve.

AFTERWORD

*I*n *The Annals of Sandy Spring*, William Henry Farquhar quoted from a circa 1820 sketch of Sandy Spring by William Darby: "Sandy Spring is one of those nooks from which we can see the stir of the great Babel, and not feel the crowd." This could still describe parts of Montgomery County today. Washington, D.C., and the down-county whirl with business and traffic, while in parts of the up-county, the only reminder of an outside world might be an occasional plane overhead.

But the country and city continue to enrich each other. As Farquhar noted, mingling slow country ways with fast city ones can "enliven the faculties" often to "mutual advantage." He noted that the "town and country are so constituted that each is necessary to the other," a fact that hasn't changed.

History echoes through the Reserve and at county tables, particularly in their diversity. Diversity can be viewed in many ways—a characteristic of the natural environment, social communities and economies. It may be seen as a threat or as a benefit, but it is surely necessary to survival.

Native plants were gathered and farmed by indigenous peoples, whose actions spread seeds and favored certain species and characteristics. Later settlers turned plants into crops—for food and to sell—through selective breeding and hybridization. Today, county farmers farm using different methods and technologies, producing commodity crops, table crops and value-added products. Those changes over time were matters of survival.

Likewise, the county's people have been diverse. Native groups passed through the county, drawn to the fish and wildlife along the Potomac

River. Early settlers adapted some farming and social patterns of their Tidewater plantation neighbors to the south and some of their German farmstead neighbors to the north. Indentured Irish workers and Scottish merchants seeking new opportunities left their mark on the county—the C&O Canal, Georgetown warehouses and innumerable community names. Enslaved laborers made county farms prosperous and later settled in strong communities that persist today.

That social diversity continues, with communities from around the world. Montgomery County's residents speak more than forty languages; county restaurants, bakeries and food businesses reflect that same variety.

Over time, the county's economy has diversified—from native trading along the river to the canal connecting ports and capital to inland farms. Farmers in the past shifted their crops from corn to wheat to dairy to meet the market, and the county's farmwomen brought their domestic skills to market in Bethesda. Farmers today grow to suit their customers. Kingsbury's Orchard specializes in Asian pears, and Land Link farms such as Passion to Seed and Dodo Farms grow a variety of organic produce for local eaters. Other local agricultural businesses focus on value-added products, like Soleado's lavender soaps, Banner Bee Company's honey and beeswax products and Rocklands' wine.

While that proximity to the capital city created opportunity—Thomas Moore invented a "refrigeratory" to bring his dairy products to market, and Bill Marriott used it to establish his business feeding office workers and expanded to worldwide hospitality; it also created tension. Land in the county was a commodity, whether it was used for agriculture or development.

Another echo of history is the way farming techniques and community are always evolving. As Quaker farmers improved their soil and formed societies to share information, today's farmers also compare notes on markets, the effects of climate change and farming policies. Many farms and businesses follow their owners' individual passions, but they also construct viable business models and see the work as meaningful contribution to the community—preserving land, providing healthy food and offering natural beauty and respite.

Food has the capacity to unite people, a way we can learn about ourselves, our neighbors and our communities. Native people helped European settlers survive by sharing farming and hunting expertise. Macie King saw a need and way to help her farming community and helped establish a market that kept her community self-reliant and thriving through the Depression. As Bill Duvall noted, "[A]t that time, farmers helped each other out, like at wheat harvest time, lots of men came, it took many hands to thresh wheat, and the ladies prepared a huge meal—the lunch was a social affair." County farmers still share expertise, labor and equipment and look out for the needs of their communities. County residents gather at the table—to eat food created by their neighbors from around the corner or around the world.

Today, we think of food literacy as encouraging people to try a kohlrabi or to notice the taste and texture of farm-raised meat and free-range eggs. In the past, food literacy was a matter of survival. Early settlers came looking to extract from the land (ore, pelts, crops and more) that could be sold. They had to learn from native peoples how to feed themselves in a new land—what could be foraged and grown most successfully. Elizabeth Ellicott Lea's cookbook was more than recipes—it was a manual to running a successful farm operation and a way to approach life.

Part of food literacy is land literacy. Preserving farmland was a deliberate act by the county, and the effort continues with programs like the Montgomery Countryside Alliance's Land Link, which connects farmers with landowners, and by advocating for policies and regulations that support farm operations. What we expect of land changes with each generation. Initial settlers looked for arable land near waterways that could power a mill or connect to a market. Today, mills are preserved in the names of streets and subdivisions, and land takes its value from what can be built on it.

Diversity—in populations, technology, land use and economies—is the key to resiliency, the ability to move quickly to respond to change. Although it took time, the initial decision to create the Agricultural Reserve had diversity and resiliency at its heart. Montgomery County's mix of land uses creates a mix of people, jobs, recreation and environments.

The next decisions are how to keep the Reserve vital for new generations. Planning decisions seek to identify the Reserve's value as an asset for the county and the region—not for development but for meaningful and innovative agriculture. While the large pattern of up-county agriculture and down-county development has proven to be resilient, new planning policies must balance farming with increasing access to down-county residents. At the same time, development regulations, community design and zoning must enable food production in unconsidered spaces—urban gardens, suburban chickens and rooftop agriculture.

In Silver Spring, the Charles Koiner Conservancy for Urban Farming sells garden produce grown on one acre in a suburban community just a few blocks from the Metro station that Charlie Koiner farmed for forty years. For Charlie, growing and selling figs, peppers, tomatoes, kale, collards and

Thanks to shared efforts, public and private, Sugarloaf Mountain and surrounding farmland remain part of Montgomery County's landscape and economy. *Courtesy George Kousoulas.*

onions to his neighbors was a passion. Today the nonprofit CKC carries on his legacy by preserving the land with a conservancy easement and continuing to farm through a lease agreement with his daughter, Lynne.

On Thursday evenings, when the farm is open for sales, it lives as a "kind of park" and a neighborhood hub, according to Hannah Sholder, founder and deputy director. Even on a drizzly evening, the corner lot is busy with volunteers working in the beds and neighbors comparing notes about favorite greens and how to cook them. Others line up for dinner from the food truck—falafel this week, Mexican street food the next. One little girl has a question for Hannah: "When will the squash be this big?" holding her hands just so. Hannah estimates five days and encourages her to take a squash plant home. Thursday evenings at the garden are an opportunity to visit with neighbors who have become regular customers and educate residents about the potential of land and local food.

Local food is often described as coming from a one-hundred-mile radius, but small farms, integrated into communities, can produce food within one mile of home. Farm manager Kara Piccirilli wants CKC to be a model for keeping food systems local, and her work includes planning the farm—crop succession, composting, planting plans—as well as changing people's expectations about food and land. Sholder pointed out that CKC farms only an eighth of the three-acre Silver Spring site but still produces about $16,000 worth of food each season. Beyond its Silver Spring site, the conservancy is working to develop new sites that integrate food production into communities on public and private lands that can expand access to food. Sholder recognizes their advantage of farming as a nonprofit entity—they can apply for grants, get public support and work with volunteers. "Farming for profit is hard"—a statement that few farmers will argue with.

CKC's land arrangement is just as complex as the one that created the Agricultural Reserve, albeit at a much smaller scale. But the first step toward preserving land for local food is recognizing and supporting the potential for growing food, whether on acres of land zoned for agriculture or on a sunny residential site. Montgomery Parks operates a Community Garden Program that sets aside gardening plots for individual households. On a total of twelve acres spread across the county, 118 small plots, about four hundred square feet, are tended by local gardeners. Michelle Nelson is the program manager and noticed that not all gardeners were doing a full harvest and so set up a trial gleaning party to gather produce that could be donated. Since 2018, the program has been formalized; the Fenton Street gardens in Silver Spring has donated five hundred pounds of produce to nearby Shepherd's Table.

The community gardens are established to grow food as a recreational option provided by the Parks Department; it required observation and cooperation to set up partnership with local communities to make the most of produce that would otherwise be wasted. A more complex and larger-scale arrangement was established with the Department's Pope Farm. This ninety-two-acre Gaithersburg site is the nursery for the plants and flowers used in county parks. In 2019, the farm grew daikon radish as a cover crop to improve soil health. Daikon's large taproot breaks up compacted soil, increasing aeration and water filtration. Nelson pointed out that it's also a low-maintenance crop, requires minimal labor and is a culturally appropriate food for some county communities. Like a large carrot, they are often pickled and stir-fried in Asian dishes. Rather than pulling and composting the vegetables, the farm staff worked in partnership with Harvestshare to harvest; Pope Farm was able to donate four thousand pounds of produce to nonprofits and residents facing food insecurity.

This was treated as a pilot program, as Nelson said, "a proof of concept," and the goal is to expand from one crop and four thousand pounds to a variety of crops twice that size. She also sees the potential for expanding the program to other sites working in cooperation with park managers, maintenance crews and the community.

That's one model of finding space for food in unanticipated places, and Calleva offers another model. This family-run summer camp has offered generations of Montgomery County children typical summer camp experiences—horseback riding, canoeing and camping—but in 1996, the Markoff family, who run the camp, purchased a farm on Martinsburg Road with the goal of developing farm-oriented adventures for people of all ages. Sustainable farming was a natural outgrowth of camp activities that were based in local forests and rivers. The farm vision grew from the goal of balancing Calleva's camp programs with the ethos of stewardship and the spirit of the Agricultural Reserve.

Over the years, Calleva Farm has developed camp programs that focus on farming. In a combination of education and fun, Growing Green campers participate in a self-sufficient farming cycle, working with animals, learning traditional growing practices and cooking and eating local. Their parents can enjoy a local food experience at Calleva Farm's seasonal Dirty Dinners, which feature a farm tour, entertainment and a local meal under the stars. The dinners are a way to highlight the Reserve as well as local growers, brewers, winemakers and artists.

These experiences feature locally grown, farm-fresh foods and the value of traditional small-scale farming and are extended into the community at the Poolesville Calleva Farm Store—stocked with the farm's produce and products from local makers.

Both Calleva and CKC provide an education that has been overlooked and are small steps toward self-sufficiency—children and their parents learning the value of local food—and support a local farm economy. And like the farmers who have preceded them in the Reserve, they have created a product and found a market for it. They are part of the county's variety of life and work made possible by the land preserved in the Agricultural Reserve.

These operations also support local food self-sufficiency. During the world wars and Depression, all community members worked to provide local food not as a matter of preference but as a matter of survival. The value of local food production was made vivid during the 2020 COVID pandemic. Broken supply chains highlighted how our food reaches us—traveling across the country and the world. Our expectations of open restaurants and full grocery shelves were upended, forcing us to be more resilient in our own kitchens. The pandemic also revealed how many of our neighbors were already facing food options limited by income, health or transportation.

The County Council established the Rustic Roads program in 1993 and implemented it through a 1996 plan, which identified the features of rustic roads, recommended new road classifications and identified scenic easement setbacks to protect scenic, historic and rural characteristics. It is a recognition that land and transportation are linked in function and aesthetics. *Courtesy George Kousoulas.*

Incorporating food production into the way we think about land and development is good for the environment, can help build a sense of community, can support neighbors and can create beautiful landscapes and delicious meals.

The historical tension between agriculture and development identified by Boyd and Scharf remains. The county anticipates 200,000 new residents over the next thirty years who will need homes, schools, parks and communities. While the large swaths of open land in the Reserve look tempting, the county has a long commitment to maintaining the Reserve as primarily for agriculture uses, recognizing its value as a place for food, jobs, environmental protection, recreation and historic preservation. Royce Hanson, Planning Board chairman and a founding planner of the Agricultural Reserve, sees its value growing and hopes that it will remain a working landscape.

While the county is committed to this stewardship, the Reserve's function, character and long-term viability will come from the details of development—road widths, allowed uses, permitting requirements—that

BIBLIOGRAPHY

Alcott, Louisa May. *Hospital Sketches*. Boston: James Redpath, 1863. http://digital.library.upenn.edu/women/alcott/sketches/sketches.html.

Armstrong, Edith M. *Days at Cabin John: A Story of Maryland Neighbors Along the Chesapeake and Ohio Canal*. New York: Vantage Press, 1958.

Boyd, T.H.S. *The History of Montgomery County, from Its Earliest Settlement*. Clarksburg, MD: W.K. Boyle & Son, 1879. http://hdl.handle.net/2027/loc.ark:/13960/t2s46xv5x.

Brooke, Mary Coffin. *Memories of Eighty Years*. New York: Knickerbocker Press, 1916. https://archive.org/details/memorieseightyy00broogoog/mode/2up.

Carson, Barbara. *Ambitious Appetites: Dining, Behavior, and Patterns of Consumption in Federal Washington*. Washington, D.C.: American Institute of Architects Press, 1990.

Cohen, Anthony. *The Underground Railroad in Montgomery County, Maryland: A History and Driving Guide*. Montgomery County, MD: Montgomery County Historical Association, 1997.

Coleman, Margaret Marshall, and Anne Dennis Lewis. *Montgomery County: A Pictorial History*. Norfolk, VA: Donning Company, 1984.

Corrigan, Mary Beth. "Enslaved and Free African-Americans in Nineteenth Century Georgetown." Washington, D.C. Humanities Council Research Report, Tudor Place, 2013. https://tudorplace.org/wp-content/uploads/2020/08/Enslaved-Free-in-early-19th-c-Georgetown_2013.pdf.

Cuttler, Dona L. *The History of Dickerson, Mouth of Monocacy, Oakland Mills, and Sugarloaf Mountain (MD)*. Bowie, MD: Heritage Books, 1999.

Dwyer, Michael. *Montgomery County Mills: A Field Guide*. Montgomery County, MD: self-published, 2012.

Farquhar, Roger Brooke. *Historic Montgomery County, Maryland: Old Homes and History*. Washington, D.C.: Judd & Detweiler, 1952.

Farquhar, William Henry. *The Annals of Sandy Spring: Twenty Years History of a Rural Community in Maryland*. Baltimore, MD: Cushings & Bailey, 1884.

Gardner, Alexander. *Gardner's Photographic Sketch Book of the Civil War*. N.p.: self-published, 1865.

Gaskins, Ruth L. *A Good Heart and a Light Hand*. N.p., 1968.

Gutheim, Frederick. *The Potomac*. Baltimore, MD: Johns Hopkins University Press, 1986.

Hanson, Royce. *Suburb, Planning Politics and the Public Interest*. Ithaca, NY: Cornell University Press, 2017.

Harris, Ann Paterson. *The Potomac Adventure*. Montgomery County, MD: self-published, 1978.

Harris, Jessica. *High on the Hog*. New York: Bloomsbury USA, 2011.

Henson, Josiah. *The Life of Josiah Henson, Formerly a Slave, Now an Inhabitant of Canada, as Narrated by Himself*. Boston: Arthur D. Phelps, 1849. https://www.gutenberg.org/ebooks/53609.

Heritage Montgomery. *African American Heritage Cookbook*. Montgomery County, MD: self-published, 2017.

Hiebert, Ray Eldon, and Richard K. MacMaster. *A Grateful Remembrance: The Story of Montgomery County, Maryland*, 1976.

Jacobs, Charles T. *Civil War Guide to Montgomery County, Maryland*. Montgomery County, MD: Montgomery County Civil War Roundtable, 1996.

Kuhns, Jamie Ferguson. *Sharp Flashes of Lightning Come from Black Clouds: The Life of Josiah Henson*. Montgomery County, MD: M-NCPPC, 2018.

Kytle, Elizabeth. *Home on the Canal*. Baltimore, MD: Johns Hopkins University Press, 1983.

———. *Time Was: A Cabin John Memory Book*. Montgomery County, MD: Cabin John Citizens' Association, 1976.

Laas, Virginia Jeans. *Wartime Washington: The Civil War Letters of Elizabeth Blair Lee*. Chicago: University of Illinois Press, 1991.

Lea, Elizabeth Ellicott. *Domestic Cookery: Useful Receipts and Hints to Young Housekeepers*. Baltimore, MD: Cushings and Bailey, 1859. https://books.google.com/books?id=ZYiWP4v_y_sC&pg=PA3&source=gbs_selected_pages&cad=3#v=onepage&q&f=false.

Lukacs, Paul. *American Vintage: The Rise of American Wine*, Boston: Houghton Mifflin Harcourt, 2000.

Malinowksi, Sharon, and Anna Sheets, eds. *The Gale Encyclopedia of Native American Tribes*. Detroit, MI: Gale Cengage, 1998.

Maryland: A Guide to the Old Line State. Federal Writers' Project, Writers' Program of the Works Project Administration. Washington, D.C.: Government Printing Office, 1940.

McPhee, John. *The Founding Fish*. New York: Farrar, Strauss & Giroux, 2002.

Offutt, William. *Bethesda: A Social History*. Bethesda, MD: Innovation Game, 1996.

Root, Waverly, and Richard deRochemont. *Eating in America: A History*. New York: William Morrow, 1976.

Scharf, Thomas J. *History of Western Maryland*. Philadelphia, PA: Louis H. Everts, 1882. https://archive.org/details/historyofwestern01scha.

Schmit, Patricia Brady, ed. *Nelly Custis Lewis's Housekeeping Book*. New Orleans, LA: Historic New Orleans, 1982.

Shapiro, Laura. *Perfection Salad, Women and Cooking at the Turn of the Century*. New York: Farrar, Strauss and Giroux, 1986.

Shaw, Horace H. *The First Maine Heavy Artillery, 1861–1865: A History of Its Part and Place in the War for the Union, with an Outline of Causes of War and Its Results to Our Country*. Portland, ME, 1903. https://books.google.com/books/about/The_First_Maine_Heavy_Artillery_1861_186.html?id=G50dAQAAMAAJ.

Sherman, Sean. *The Sioux Chef's Indigenous Kitchen*. Minneapolis: University of Minnesota Press, 2017.

Smith, Andrew F., ed. *Oxford Companion to American Food and Drink*. New York: Oxford University Press, 2007.

Soderberg, Susan Cooke. *A Guide to Civil War Sites in Maryland: Blue and Gray in a Border State*. Shippensburg, PA: White Mane Publishing, 2011.

Sugarland Ethno-History Project. *I Have Started for Canaan*. Montgomery County, MD: Primedia eLaunch LLC, 2020.

Thom, William Taylor. *Negroes of Sandy Spring, Maryland*. Washington, D.C.: Department of Labor (Bulletin), 1899. https://www.loc.gov/resource/lcrbmrp.t8050/?sp=7.

Troiano, Edna M. *Uncle Tom's Journey from Maryland to Canada: The Life of Josiah Henson*. Charleston, SC: The History Press, 2019.

Twitty, Michael. "Shad, Fried Chicken and Apple Butter: The Foodways of Historic Montgomery County." *Montgomery County Story* 52, no. 3 (Fall/Winter 2009).

Veit, Helen Zoe. *Food in the Civil War Era: The South*. East Lansing: Michigan State University Press, 2015.

Watkins, Mrs. Spencer, and Mrs. Francis F. Field. *The Up-to-Date Cookbook of Tested Recipes*. Washington, D.C.: National Publishing Company, 1897. https://archive.org/details/uptodatecookbook00watk.

Weaver, William Woys. *A Quaker Woman's Cookbook: The Domestic Cookery of Elizabeth Ellicott Lea*. Mechanicsburg, PA: Stackpole Books, 2004.

Welles, Judith. *Cabin John: Legends and Life of an Uncommon Place*. Montgomery County, MD: Cabin John Citizens' Association, 2008.

———. *Potomac*. Charleston, SC: Arcadia Publishing, 2019.

INDEX

ABOUT THE AUTHORS

 CLAUDIA KOUSOULAS worked as a land-use planner for more than twenty years in Montgomery County, Maryland, and is also a freelance writer and editor whose topics include architecture, urbanism, food culture and culinary history. She is the coauthor of *Bread and Beauty: A Year in Montgomery County's Agricultural Reserve*.

ELLEN LETOURNEAU is a fiber artist, baker and event planner. As a member of the Common Grain Alliance and Chesapeake Fibershed, she is interested in the revival of grain and fiber economies in the region, and she is also the coauthor of *Bread and Beauty: A Year in Montgomery County's Agricultural Reserve*.